WHO IS THE HOLY SPIRIT?
The Truth Will Surprise You
By: Jay Whitaker

Copyright © 2019, 2021

Paperback ISBN: 978-1-7343602-8-8
Hardcover ISBN: 978-1-7343602-1-9
eBook ISBN: 978-1-7343602-3-3

Cover design by Exodus Design Studios

Printed in the United States of America

Second Edition: September 2020
Revised: February 2021

# TABLE OF CONTENTS

# DEDICATION

I would like to dedicate this book to my wife Rowena, the Love of my Life. She has always supported me and encouraged me to Believe, to keep Walking out this Revelation, and to keep Walking out our Faith; even when the path became steep, she has always been there, walking beside me.

I love you Baby!

# ACKNOWLEDGMENT

There are a few people we would like to mention that have been instrumental in our Walk, who we would like to thank and recognize as it says in the Word: "Give honor where honor is due" Irma & Jesse Molina, and Paul & Linda Nones, are all very dear friends of ours and have been essential in the Spiritual Development of both Rowena, and me. Thank you for stepping out in faith, and thank you for always being willing to share your wisdom and your prayers with us.

Additionally, I would like to mention my good friend, Bill Lancaster, who was the Best Man at our Wedding, and will continue to be our life-long friend.

Renz & Julie Roldan, and Patrick De Vera, who we have shared our faith with, and this Revelation, and who will become the Spiritual Leaders of the future, and Guides to the Youth of this world.

And finally, we would like to thank our parents, who planted the seeds of our faith and helped us grow into the people we are today. We love you, Mom & Les, Liliana & Dad, Nanay & Tatay.

***Thank you for always being there for us.***

# INTRODUCTION

My name is Jay Whitaker, and I was born in San Antonio, Texas, USA, in 1962. I had lived in California for most of my life, up until 2018, when we made Washington State our home. I have been a Spirit-Filled, Born-Again Christian since the age of 27, back in 1990, when a co-worker – and now dear friend – Paul Nones, shared his testimony with me, witnessed to me, and introduced me to Jesus as my Lord and Savior. In the years that followed, I thought I had come to a pretty good understanding of who the GODHEAD was, since even before I was Born-Again, I was raised Catholic and had often heard the phrase, "In the name of the Father, the Son, and the Holy Spirit." But, when I thought deeply about that relationship, something never made sense to me, although I had never really taken the time to investigate it. I would ask myself, "Could the GODHEAD really be comprised of Three Males?" and "How could Jesus really be the '*First Born*' of GOD?" Over the years, I had come across many Old Testament and New Testament Scriptures stating how The LORD GOD felt about marital relationships, as well as other Scriptures referring to how marriage is between a man and woman, and the blessing of the children they produced. So, how could this be? The New Testament reinforces this idea about marriage and GOD's Character, and even Jesus describes us Believers as the "*Bride of Christ*", and that Jesus is "*the same yesterday, today, and forever*".

Any time I would think deeply about this topic, so many thoughts would go through my mind, but nothing ever really made any sense to me, so ultimately, I would just end up being even more confused than when I started, and would just give up… that is, until early 2018, when I had a Revelation.

# CHAPTER ONE

# CHALLENGING OUR TRADITIONS

Before we dive into the topic of the Holy Spirit, I wanted to share something important I have learned that is directly related to our ability to really grab hold of this Revelation about the Holy Spirit.

Here it is…

## "Our Traditions can interfere with GOD's Truth"

Most people assume they know and can recognize "Truth" when they hear it, but it may not be "GOD's Truth". Jesus declares this plainly to us in Matthew 15 when He tells us:

### _Matthew 15:1-3,6-9_
*Then the Scribes and Pharisees who were from Jerusalem came to Jesus, saying, "Why do Your Disciples violate the Traditions of the elders? **Jesus answered and said to them, "Why do you violate the Commandments of GOD because of your Traditions? By doing this, you have made the Words of GOD worthless by your Traditions! Hypocrites! Very well did Isaiah Prophesy about you, saying:***

*'**These people come near to Me with the words of their mouth, and honor Me with their lips, but their heart is far from Me. And in vain they worship Me, teaching in its place as doctrines, the commandments of men.' "***

Let me give you a few more examples in Scripture to show that our preconceived ideas can actually interfere with GOD's Truth. Just bear with me while we Walk this out, and I promise it will make perfect sense to you when we are finished.

According to the text of the Bible, how many Apostles were there in total? You likely said 12, right? Well, actually, there were a total of 14. Now you are probably thinking, "Wait! What is this guy talking about?" Well, there were 12 Original, then the Apostles added 1 (named Matthias), and Jesus added 1 (named Paul)

But, in reality, this is what actually happened: There were 12 Apostles until Judas killed himself… then there were 11. We then read in Acts 1, that Jesus met up with these same 11 Apostles on the Mount of Olives, that "*He had Chosen*", right before He ascended and told them not to leave Jerusalem until after they received Power from the Holy Spirit, which we know came later during Pentecost, as was described in Acts 2.

*Acts 1:2,4-5*
*Jesus had given Commandments to **the Apostles whom He had chosen**… On one occasion, while Jesus was with them, He gave them this Command: "Do not leave Jerusalem, but **wait for the Promise of the Father**; that which you have heard Me say, 'For John truly baptized with water, but **you will be baptized with the Holy Spirit**.' not many days from now."*

Do we read that Jesus also told them to pick a replacement for Judas? No! The Apostles went back to their house in Jerusalem, and *they decided* that while they were waiting they would just replace Judas, which they did by Rolling Dice, referred to as "*Casting Lots*" back then, but, they were not told to do this by Jesus, nor by the Holy Spirit since Pentecost had not yet come… so why did they do this?

They did this because of something *they thought* might apply to them. They then narrowed it down to two guys and let the Dice decide. These Dice ultimately chose Matthias, who, in reality, was never heard from again in the Bible.

Can you imagine choosing a Pastor of a Church this way? The Board of Directors of a Church all gather around and decide that the best way to select a new Pastor for their Church would be to give it over to "Chance", by a Roll of the Dice.

That idea sounds absurd, right? Well, that is precisely what they did. Only it was much worse than that because they decided that they were just as qualified to choose an Apostle as Jesus was. But, what happens a little later on in Acts 9? We read that Jesus personally shows up again to "Choose" Paul to replace Judas, in the same way that Jesus had chosen His other Apostles... in person! And, we all know just how much Paul accomplished, in addition to writing the majority of the New Testament.

It is interesting to note that we later read in Revelation 21:12, referring to the New Jerusalem City that will come down from Heaven, it says, "*Now the wall of the City had 12 foundations, and on them were the names of the 12 Apostles of the Lamb.*" It doesn't say 13 or 14; it says 12 Apostles, and they belonged to Jesus "*the Lamb*". So, what does all this really mean?

The point is this: They didn't ask, and they used their own understanding and their own "Traditions" to replace Judas. Do you see where I'm going with this now? Let me give you a few more examples, but these will revolve around the Birth of Jesus.

Now this next part may actually shake some of you up, but the Birth of Jesus did not occur in December, it was actually in March or April, which is the Jewish month of "Nisan", when at the same time – and only time of the year – all the Shepherds live and sleep in the fields with the Sheep to watch over the Birth of the Sacrificial Lambs for the Temple. Do you remember that John the Baptist called Jesus "*the Lamb of GOD who takes away the sin of the world*" in John 1:29? We also see this clearly in 1 Peter 1:19, where we read plainly, "*You were bought with the precious Blood of Jesus Christ's death. He was a pure and perfect sacrificial Lamb.*" Let's now look at the account in Luke 2 below and see if the timing of why and when the Shepherds were living in the fields becomes clearer.

*Luke 2:8-12*
*Now **there were Shepherds in the same region of Galilee, who were living out in the fields, keeping watch over their flock by night.** And an Angel of the LORD stood before them, and the glory of the LORD shone around them, and they were greatly afraid. Then the Angel said to them, "Do not be afraid, for behold, I bring you good tidings of great Joy which will be to all people, for **there is born to you this day** in the City of David, a Savior, who is the Messiah, the Lord. And this will be the sign to you: **You will find a Baby** wrapped in swaddling clothes, lying **in a Manger.**"*

There are many more details to support His Birth in the Jewish Month of "Nisan", but it would take much too long to review it. Jonathon Cahn did an incredibly detailed video about this topic from a Jewish perspective. I would truly suggest you watch it. You can find it on YouTube at  https://youtu.be/ptlsXtTf6n0  and is titled "When Was Jesus Really Born??" To be crystal clear, this is not an endorsement for the Bakkers, but Jonathon Cahn is a Jewish man who became a Christian, who is a world-renowned Author that does an incredible job of teaching us Christianity from a Jewish historical perspective, and also operates in the Prophetic.

Another example is that the Bible does not state that there were "Three" Wise Men; it uses the plural Greek word "Maggi", meaning that there was simply more than one Wise Man. Many people just "Assume" there are three because of the three gifts of *"Gold, Frankincense, and Myrrh"*. Therefore, this idea has spread and been shared again and again over the years.

Additionally, and contrary to all the Nativity Scenes you have ever seen, the Wise Men did not arrive in the Stables at the time when Mary gave Birth; they arrived at Mary & Joseph's House around 1 to 2 years later, as shown in Matthew 2 below.

*Matthew 2:1-2,9-11*
*Now **after Jesus was born** in Bethlehem of Judea in the days of Herod the king, behold, **Wise Men** (Maggi) **from the East came to Jerusalem**, saying, **"Where is He who has been born King of the Jews? For we have seen His Star in the East and have come to worship Him."** When Herod the king heard this, he was troubled, and all Jerusalem with him. And when he had gathered all the chief Priests and Scribes of the people together, he inquired of them where the Messiah was to be born. So, they said to him, "In Bethlehem of Judea, for thus it is written by the Prophet:*
*'But you, Bethlehem, in the land of Judah, are not the least among the rulers of Judah; for out of you shall come a Ruler who will shepherd My people Israel.' "*

*Then Herod, when he had secretly called the Wise Men, determined from them **what time the Star appeared**. And*

*he sent them to Bethlehem and said, "Go and search*
*carefully for the **<u>Young Child</u>**, and when you have found*
*Him, bring back word to me, that I may come and worship*
*Him also." When they heard the king, they departed; and*
*behold, **the Star which they had seen in the East went***
*before them, till it came and stood over where the <u>Young</u>***
*<u>Child</u> was.** When they saw the Star, they rejoiced with*
*exceedingly great Joy. And **when they had come into <u>the</u>***
*<u>House</u>, they saw the <u>Young Child</u>** with Mary His mother,*
*and fell down and worshiped Him. And when they had*
*opened their treasures, they presented gifts to Him: Gold,*
*Frankincense, and Myrrh.*

The Maggi decided to take their Journey from the East only after the Star showed up to announce the Birth of Jesus. It makes sense that it would have taken them around 1 to 2 years to prepare and then travel the long journey to Israel from the East. When they finally arrived in Jerusalem, they asked *"Where is <u>He who has been born…</u>?"* since they already knew they would be looking for the location where Jesus was living, as He had already *"been born"* based on the timing of the Star they were following, just as they had told King Herod.

We read in Matthew 2 the phrase *"Young Child"* was used, which actually means "Toddler" in Greek, and is not the Greek word for *"Baby"*, as clearly shown at the time of His Birth, when we read Luke 2:12 (page 10). Therefore, the Wise Men visited a Young Child in a House, not a Baby in a Manger; the Shepherds were the ones who went to see a Baby in a Manger, as directed by the Angel.

And, do you recall that King Herod ordered to kill *"all boys two years old and under"* based on when the Star showed up in the sky? Why would Herod do that if Jesus were a Baby that had just been born? This description of *"two years old and under"* is very consistent with the Greek word for *"Young Child"* used above.

Ok, here is my last example, then I will explain why all this matters:

Most people think that Noah took 2 of every type of animal into the Ark, a male and a female. This is not entirely accurate. The Scripture, in fact, does say that he took 2 of each of the *"unclean animals"*, but 14 of each of the *"clean animals"*, and 14 of *"every kind of bird"*. You can find this in Genesis 7.

So, what is the point of all this?

Well, we often get so set in our Traditions, and the things we have heard or seen from others in the past, that we don't search it out for ourselves, to indeed know GOD's Truth. We all need to simply read the Word of GOD for ourselves, and Seek out the Wisdom that only comes from GOD, and then we will all know GOD's Truth, not merely "truth" that is based on our own personal understanding.

Jesus said this to us in Luke 11…

*"I say to you, ask, and keep asking, and it will be given to you; seek, and keep seeking, and you will find; knock, and keep knocking, and it will be opened to you. For everyone who asks receives, and he who seeks finds, and to him who knocks it will be opened."*

We need to be open to the idea that most of us may have blinders on when it comes to hearing something new and unusual. We must not allow our Traditions to stop us from becoming all that GOD wants us to become for the Kingdom of Heaven, as Solomon said plainly to us in Proverbs 3…

*Proverbs 3:5*
*"Do not lean on your understanding."*

We can also see in Acts 17 that Luke, in fact, complemented the Bereans for their proper response to hearing something new from Paul and Silas. At that time, Paul & Silas were also sharing a new Revelation that the Bereans had never heard before.

*Acts 17:11*
*"These in Berea were more **fair-minded** than those in Thessalonica, in that they **received the Word with all readiness**, and **searched the Scriptures** daily to find out **whether these things were true**."*

They didn't just say, "Oh, that's too strange, so I'm not even going to bother looking into that!" They took the time and looked it up in the Word of GOD for themselves.

Unfortunately, some people believe that the Bible is fully completed, and that GOD will do nothing new, aside from what has already happened or been written about. These same people often will use Revelation 22 to justify it, saying that you cannot add or subtract from "the Bible", simply because someone decided to place the Book of Revelation at the end of the Bible.

*Revelation 22:18-19*
*For I testify to everyone who hears **the words** of the Prophecy of **this book**: **If anyone adds to these words**, GOD will add to him the plagues that are written in this book; and **if anyone takes away from the words of the book of this Prophecy**, GOD shall take away his part from the Tree of Life, from the Holy City, and from the things which are written in this book.*

You can clearly see that what John was actually warning us about was adding or taking away from "*the Book of Revelation*", not from the 66 books that comprise the modern Bible, which, in fact, at that time had not yet even been "assembled by man". The Bible, as we know it today, came 1400 years later.

Ready for some more examples? Well, several Books are missing from the Bible! I can already hear some of you thinking, "What!? Missing Books? No Way!" Well, it's true!

In Colossians 4:16, Paul writes, "*Now when this Epistle* (the Book of Colossians) *is read among you, see that it is also read in the Church of the Laodiceans, and that you likewise read **the Epistle from Laodicea**.*" How many of you have ever seen the *Book of Laodiceans* in the Bible? No? Me neither! It is missing!

Also, there are "Extra-Biblical Books" that we already know about, and are either missing, or not included in the Bible. Jesus, the Apostles, and other writers quote from many of these other Books that are not in the Bible, like the Book of Enoch, the Book of Jubilees, and the Book of Jasher which is also mentioned in Joshua 10:13. Enoch is quoted by several writers and actually mentioned by name in the New Testament as an example of a great man of Faith. Crazy, right?

Well, with all that said, that is why I truly believe in something referred to as "Progressive Revelation"… meaning that the GODHEAD will continue to reveal more and more about "Themselves" over time, including "Their Nature", and "Their Kingdom". An excellent example of this comes to us in Exodus 6 below, and shows us that the LORD GOD had revealed more about "Their Nature" when They revealed the new Name that They were now to be known by, but had not been known by that Name in the past.

*Exodus 6:2-3*
*And **GOD** (Elohim) **spoke to Moses** and said to him: "**I am the LORD** (YHWH). I appeared to Abraham, to Isaac, and to Jacob, as God Almighty (El Shaddai), but by **My Name LORD** (YHWH) **I was not known to them**."*

Do you recall in the Book of Acts, that during Pentecost, many people thought the Apostles and Disciples were drunk or insane when the Holy Spirit was first poured out? New things can seem very strange at first!

Daniel 12 states plainly about how in the *"End Times"* we will all see that *"Knowledge will increase"*. How can that happen if we already know everything we are going to know? Jesus supports this when He says in John 14:

16

*John 14:12*
*"Truly, truly, I say to you, <u>whoever believes in Me will</u>*
*<u>also do the Works that I do; and even Greater Works than</u>*
*<u>these will they do</u>, because I am going to the Father."*


That is amazing!  Although it hasn't happened yet… it will, because the Words of Jesus are Truth.

Well, this is precisely the type of thing you are about to hear from me… many new things you have most likely never heard before, so you will need to keep an open mind, and search the Scriptures yourselves for GOD's Truth.  Is everybody Ready?  Well here goes…


A few years ago, I was given a series of powerful Revelations about the Holy Spirit… these Revelations shook me to my foundation; they changed me, and my Christian Walk, forever.

Over the past 30 years of my being a Christian, and after all this time since I first heard this, including all the research I have done since then, I have never heard from anyone what I am about to share with you now.

One day, while I was reading the Book of Luke, as I had so many times before, I came across the phrase, *"The Holy Spirit will come upon you, and the Power of the Most High will overshadow you; therefore, also, that Holy One who is to be born will be called the Son of GOD."* and it was as if a bright light went on in my mind; like GOD just did a download directly into my Soul.  So many Scriptures came flooding into my mind at the same time, not only focused on the GODHEAD, but more specifically, on who the Holy Spirit truly is.

17

Do you remember what I said about our own Traditions and our own understandings?  Well, my first thought regarding what I had heard was that it was such a crazy notion, it could not possibly be true.  So, because of these Revelations, and my questions, I spent the next couple of years researching and documenting all the information I received about the Holy Spirit.  I then compiled it all into this Book.

I have come to understand that these Revelations were given to show the true nature of our LORD GOD, meaning the Trinity, or the GODHEAD, which includes the Father, the Son, and the Holy Spirit.  These Revelations are also focused on our relationship to Them… meaning exactly _who_ we are in the Kingdom of Heaven.

So, what I am hoping to share with you now, is that Revelation, based on the Scriptures shared with me at that time, as well as many, many others, in the sincere hope that you will come to see GOD, and more specifically, the Holy Spirit, in an entirely new, and quite honestly, an exciting new way.

_1 Peter 3:15_
_Always be prepared to give an answer to anyone who asks_
_you to give the reason for the Hope that you have in you._
_But do this with gentleness and respect._

So, let's Walk this out together, but first, let me lay down some much needed groundwork, by going over some relevant background information…

# CHAPTER TWO

# WHO IS THE GODHEAD?

Most often throughout the Bible, the GODHEAD is referred to as "*The LORD GOD*", and is first mentioned in Genesis 2:4 referring to the Creation account; originally written in Hebrew as ( יְהוָה אֱלֹהִים ) which is written right to left, and is translated as (YHWH Elohim), but is written in English as "*LORD GOD*". What is interesting is that YHWH is not just the word for "*LORD*"… it is also GOD's Name.

*Genesis 2:4*
*This is the history of the Heavens and the Earth when they were created, **in the day that The LORD GOD made the Earth and the Heavens**…*

*Exodus 3:15*
*Moreover, GOD said to Moses, "Thus you shall say to the children of Israel: '**The LORD GOD** (YHWH Elohim) of your fathers, the God of Abraham, the God of Isaac, and the God of Jacob, has sent me to you. **This is My Name forever**, and this is My memorial to all generations.' "*

*Exodus 6:2-3*
*And GOD (Elohim) **spoke to Moses** and said to him: "**I am the LORD** (YHWH). I appeared to Abraham, to Isaac, and to Jacob, as God Almighty (El Shaddai), **but by My Name LORD** (YHWH) **I was not known to them**."*

Most people, when verbally trying to speak GOD's Name, will say, Yahweh, Yahveh, Yehovah, or Jehovah, but none of these are technically correct as far as we know. You see, the original Hebrew word YHWH ( יְהֹוָה ) is made up of four letters, which can be consonants or vowels. The actual pronunciation has been lost for many generations. People have assumed that they are all consonants, and then just added the vowels from the Hebrew word "Adonai", meaning *"Lord"* in plural form, like the plural word Elohim, which they did out of intense Reverence, but also out of fear, to avoid mispronouncing GOD's true Name. Many of the Jewish people to this day will simply say, "Ha-Shem" which means "The Name", and is used as a substitute, so as not to say it incorrectly.

The word for "GOD", used in the phrase "LORD GOD", is the word "Elohim" in Hebrew, and is pronounced "El-o-heem". This word is the plural form of the singular word for *"God"*, which is "El", as in the phrase "El Shaddai", meaning *"God Almighty"*, as we just read in Exodus 6:3. This distinction, I believe, is expressed in this way so we can better understand the plurality of GOD, meaning that GOD is made up of three distinct Persons, although One GOD... or rather One LORD GOD. All throughout the Bible, there are specific attributes that are accredited to each of these three separate Persons, meaning the Father, the Son, and the Holy Spirit. This book will largely focus on the *"Spirit of GOD"*, primarily known in the New Testament as the *"Holy Spirit"*. The phrase *"Spirit of GOD"* was first used in Genesis 1 in describing the Creation of all things.

*Genesis 1:1-2*
*In the beginning, **GOD created the Heavens and the Earth.**
Now the Earth was formless and empty, darkness was over
the surface of the deep, and the **Spirit of GOD** was hovering
over the waters.*

# NOTE:

You may have already noticed I have used different ways to write the words relating to our God. Different versions of the Bible show this in several ways. Some do nothing to distinguish the difference between these words, while others do very similar. I have found it difficult to differentiate between these different words, once translated to English from the original Hebrew and Greek, if this is not done. Here are the spellings and meanings you will find throughout my writings, which I have reviewed and confirmed for myself from the original Hebrew and Greek.

- LORD: YHWH – The Name of the One and only true God, the God of Abraham, Isaac, and Jacob; the Name of our Creator. (See also: Jeremiah 33:2, Amos 5:8, & Amos 9:6)

- Lord: As in the Lord Jesus, meaning He is the sovereign ruler over us, and all that we have is His. It also can refer to the Father in His role as The Sovereign King seated on The Highest Throne in Heaven.

- lord: As in a man who is a leader and has charge over others, and usually has some Human nobility.

- GOD: Elohim, the Plural GODHEAD, the Triune GOD; the Father, the Son, and the Holy Spirit together as One.

- God: El, the positional title, meaning our God, our One Deity, the One we worship.

- god: A deity that people worship, other than The LORD GOD, like an Idol or statue, a Demon, or other false gods.

- Spirit: The Holy Spirit, the Spirit of GOD, or The Spirit.

- spirit: Our spirit, as in a Human being; other spiritual beings, a spirit, as in an Angel or Demon.

You will also note I have **Highlighted sections of Scripture with Blue**. This is done to give specific emphasis to the topic and should be given more attention. But to get the entire picture of what the Scriptures are really saying, it is essential for you to read all of the Verses in their entirety, and not just the highlighted sections.

I have also placed brackets around (*added relevant information*) in the Scriptures and elsewhere to provide additional information that will help you to fully understand the topics of discussion.

Now, getting back to the Revelation that first started me on this journey. The Scripture that triggered all of this was spoken by the Angel Gabriel to Mary.

### *Luke 1:35*
*"The Holy Spirit will come upon you, and the Power of the Most High will overshadow you; therefore, also, that Holy One who is to be born will be called the Son of GOD."*

I often wondered why this particular Revelation might have come through Luke, but, being he was a Medical Doctor and a Disciple of Jesus Christ, the Messiah, this made perfect sense to me after I Walked this out. You will come to understand later on why I say this as the Revelation becomes clearer. This story's context is when Mary first found out she was going to become pregnant and give Birth to the Son of GOD, who was to be named Jesus.

*Luke 1:26-38*

*Now in the sixth month of Elizabeth's pregnancy, **the Angel Gabriel** was sent by GOD to a City of Galilee named Nazareth, to a Virgin Engaged to be married to a man whose name was Joseph, a descendant of King David. **The Virgin's name was Mary. The Angel went to her and said**, "Rejoice, highly favored one, the LORD is with you; blessed are you among women!" Mary was greatly troubled at his words and wondered what kind of greeting this was. Then the Angel said to her, "Do not be afraid Mary, for you have found favor with GOD. And behold, you will conceive in your womb and bring forth a Son, and shall call His name Jesus. He will be great, and will be called the **Son of the Highest**; and The LORD GOD will give Him the throne of His father David. And He will reign over the house of Jacob forever, and of His Kingdom, there will be no end." Then Mary said to the Angel, "How can this be, since I have not been with a man before?" And the Angel answered and said to her, "**The Holy Spirit** will come upon you, **and** the Power of the **Most High** will overshadow you; therefore, also, that Holy One who is to be born will be called the Son of GOD. Now indeed, Elizabeth, your cousin, has also conceived a son* (John the Baptist) *in her old age; and this is now the sixth month for her who was called barren. For with GOD, nothing will be impossible." Then Mary said, "Behold the maidservant of the LORD! Let it be to me according to your word." And the Angel departed from her.*

Wait!  Gabriel just said the Holy Spirit <u>AND</u> the Most High!  Yes, you read that right.

So, who is "*the Most High*"?

To understand this concept better, you will need to appreciate how a Monarchy works. The Kingdom of GOD is a perfect and absolute Monarchy. Terms like: King, Prince, Throne, Crown, and Lord are all familiar within the context of a Monarchy and are used extensively throughout the Bible, but what Term seems to be missing from the Bible? I will get into that detail much more later on...

But for now, and before we get into the specific Revelation that I was given about the Holy Spirit, we will need to determine who *"the Most High"* or *"the Highest"* really is? Well, according to the Bible, this designation is attributed to the Father. You see, Jesus and the Holy Spirit both refer to the Father in Their accounts of His being seated on The Throne in Heaven, and although they are co-equals as GOD, they have placed themselves in the position of being in submission to Him. In the Scriptures below, you can see that Jesus considers His Father as *"the only true God"* and is also *"greater than I am"*. Paul describes the Father as not only the Father of Jesus, but One who is also *"His God"*. The Holy Spirit is *"sent"* by the Father, in the name of His Son Jesus. All these Scriptures show us a level of submission to the Father by both Jesus and the Holy Spirit. These Scriptures, and others, clearly show us the Father as being the <u>Most</u> High or rather the Highest level out of the three of Them.

### *Isaiah 6:1-3*
*... **I saw the Lord** (the Father) **sitting on a Throne, high and lifted up, and the train of His robe filled the Temple.** Above it stood Seraphim; each one had six wings: with two he covered his face, with two he covered his feet, and with two he flew. And one cried to another and said: "**Holy, Holy, Holy** (Three in One) **is the LORD of hosts; the whole Earth is full of Their Glory!**"*

*John 14:28,31*

Jesus speaking: *"You have heard Me say to you, 'I am going away and coming back to you.' If you loved Me, you would rejoice because I am going to the Father, **for the Father is <u>greater than I am</u>.** But that the world may know that I love the Father, **whatever the Father gives Me Commandment to do, that is what I do."***

*Ephesians 1:1-23*

*Paul, an Apostle of Jesus, the Messiah, by the Will of GOD, to the Believers who are in Ephesus, and faithful in Christ Jesus: Grace to you and Peace from God our Father and the Lord Jesus, the Messiah.*

**Blessed be <u>the God</u> and Father <u>of our Lord Jesus</u> Christ,** *who has blessed us with every spiritual blessing in the heavenly places in the Messiah, just as He chose us in Him before the foundation of the world, that we should be holy and without blame before Him in love, having predestined us to adoption as sons and heirs through Jesus, the Messiah, to Himself, according to the delight of His Will, to the praise of the Glory of His Grace, by which He bestowed upon us in the One whom He loves, in whom we have redemption through His Blood, the forgiveness of sins, according to the riches of His Grace which He lavished upon us in all Wisdom and Understanding, having made known to us the Mystery of His Will, according to His delight which He purposed in Himself, that in the administration of the completion of the times He might gather together in one, all things in the Messiah, that which is in Heaven and which are on Earth, in Him whom also we have obtained an inheritance, being predestined according to the purpose of Him who works all things according to the counsel of His Will, that we who first trusted in the Messiah should be to the praise of His Glory.*

*In Him you also trusted, after you heard the Word of Truth, the Gospel of your salvation; in whom also, having believed, you were sealed with **the Holy Spirit of Promise, who is the assurance of our inheritance** until the redemption of the purchased possession, to the praise of His Glory.*

*Therefore I also, after I heard of your Faith in the Lord Jesus and your love for all the Believers, do not cease to give thanks for you, making mention of you in my prayers: that **the God of our Lord Jesus Christ, the Father of Glory, may give to you the Spirit of Wisdom** (Holy Spirit) and Revelation in the Knowledge of Him, the eyes of your hearts being enlightened; that you may know what is the Hope of His Calling, what are the riches of the Glory of His inheritance in the Believers, and what is the exceeding greatness of His Power toward us who believe, according to the working of His mighty Power which He worked in the Messiah when **He** (the Father) **raised Him** (Jesus) **from the dead and seated Him at His right-hand** (on the Throne to the right of the Father's Throne) **in the heavenly places,** far above all principality and authority and power and dominion, and every name that is named, not only in this age but also in that which is to come. And He put all things under His feet, and gave Him to be head over all things to the Church, which is His Body, the fullness of Him who fills all in all.*

### Acts 1:4-8

*On one occasion, while Jesus was with them, He gave them this Command: "Do not leave Jerusalem, but wait for **the Promise of the Father*** (because the Father had promised Jesus that He would send the Holy Spirit after Jesus left to go back home); *that which you have heard Me say, 'For John truly baptized with water, but you will be baptized with **the Holy Spirit.'** not many days from now."*

*Therefore, when they had come together, they asked Him, saying, "Lord, will You at this time, restore The Kingdom to Israel?" And He said to them, "It is not for you to know times or seasons which the Father has put in His own Authority. But you shall receive Power when the Holy Spirit has come upon you, and you shall be My witnesses in Jerusalem, and in all Judea and Samaria, and to the end of the Earth."*

*John 17:1-26*

*Jesus spoke these words, lifted up His eyes to Heaven, and said: "Father, the hour has come. Glorify Your Son, that Your Son also may glorify You, as You have given Him Authority over all flesh, that He may give Eternal Life to as many as You have given Him. And this is Eternal Life, that they may know You, the only true God, and Jesus, the Messiah, whom You have sent. I have glorified You on the Earth.*

*I have finished the work which You have given Me to do. And now, O Father, glorify Me together with Yourself, with the Glory which I had with You before the world even existed.*

*I have revealed Your Name to the men whom You have given Me out of the world. They were Yours, You gave them to Me, and they have kept Your Word. Now they have known that all things which You have given Me are from You. For I have given to them the words which You have given Me; and they have received them, and have known surely that I came forth from You, and they have believed that You sent Me. I pray concerning them. I do not pray concerning the world, but concerning those whom You have given Me, for they are Yours. And all Mine are Yours, and Yours are Mine, and I am glorified in them. Now I am no longer in the world, but these are in the world, and I am coming to You.* **Holy Father, keep them in Your Name, those whom You have given Me, that they may be one as We are One.** *While I am with them, I am keeping them in* **Your Name.** *Those whom You gave Me I have guarded, and none of them is lost except the son of destruction* (Judas Iscariot), *that the Scripture might be fulfilled. But now I come to You, and these things I speak in the world, that they may have My Joy fulfilled in themselves.* **I have given them Your Word;** *and the world has hated them because they are not of the world, just as I am not of the world. I do not pray that You should take them out of the world, but that You should keep them from the Evil One. They are not of the world, just as I am not of the world. Sanctify them by Your Truth. Your Word is Truth.* **As You sent Me into the world,** *I also have sent them into the world. And for their sakes, I sanctify Myself, that they also may be sanctified by the truth.*

*I do not ask for these alone, but also for those who believe in Me, through the words of those in Me* (all Believers throughout time); *that they all may be one, as You, Father, are in Me, and I in You; that they also may be one in Us, that the world may believe that You sent Me. And the Glory which You gave Me I have given them, that they may be one just as We are One: I in them, and You in Me; that they may be made perfect in one, and that the world may know that You have sent Me, and have loved them as You have loved Me.* **Father, I desire that they also whom You gave Me may be with Me where I am, that they may behold My Glory which You have given Me; for You loved Me before the foundation of the world. O righteous Father!** *The world has not known You, but I have known You, and these have known that You sent Me. And I have declared to them Your Name, and will declare it, that the Love with which You loved Me may be in them, and I in them."*

## Mark 13:32-33

Jesus speaking: *"But of that day and hour **no one knows**, not even the Angels in Heaven, **nor the Son, but only the Father**. Take heed, watch and pray; for you do not know when the time is."*

## Luke 10:21-22

*In that hour, **Jesus rejoiced in the Holy Spirit and said, "I praise You, Father, Lord of Heaven and Earth**, that You have hidden these things from the wise and intelligent and revealed them to Babes. Even so, Father, for so it seemed good in Your sight. **All things have been delivered to Me by My Father, and no one knows who the Son is except the Father, and who the Father is except the Son, and those to whom the Son wishes to reveal Him to."***

## Matthew 28:18-20

*And Jesus came and spoke to them, saying, "**All Authority has been given to Me in Heaven** and on Earth. Go therefore and make Disciples of all the Nations, **baptizing them in the name of the Father and of the Son and of the Holy Spirit**, teaching them to observe all things that I have commanded you; and know, I am with you always, even to the end of the age." Amen.*

## John 14:25-27

Jesus speaking: *"All this I have spoken while still with you. But **the Comforter, the Holy Spirit, whom the Father will send** in My name, will teach you all things and will remind you of everything I have said to you. Peace I leave with you; My Peace I give you. I do not give to you as the world gives. Do not let your hearts be troubled and do not be afraid."*

Now, throughout all those Scriptures, we can clearly see that *The Father* is the One who is the "*Most High*" of Elohim, so let's get back to Luke 1:35… "*The Holy Spirit will come upon you, **and** the Power of the Most High will overshadow you; therefore, also, that Holy One who is to be born will be called the Son of GOD.*"

Ok, now that means *The Holy Spirt* - AND - *The Father* were both present in Mary when Jesus was conceived. But, if they are the same Person… why say they were both there separately? If they are both Male, as most people say, then how can they both be present in Mary during the conception of Jesus?

We can see that this was important enough to show us all that The Holy Spirit - AND - The Father were both present when Mary conceived. So why would this be important? Do you recall all the *other* "misconceptions" I shared earlier about the Birth of Jesus? Well, keep that in mind now…

The Revelation I had received is that Mary was not technically the Mother of Jesus – she was the Surrogate mother who carried Him – the Holy Spirit is the true Mother of Jesus!

Now I realize that many of you just thought to yourselves, "What!? I've never heard that before!" Well, that was my first thought too, and I was told this directly by the Holy Spirit. Ok, so let's Walk this out using Scripture – The Words of GOD – to prove out this Revelation as True or False. After all, what does the Scripture say about any new Revelation we receive? Do you recall earlier when we read that Luke complimented the Bereans for their proper response to hearing something new from Paul and Silas? This was a Revelation that they had never heard before either.

So, let's find out whether this makes sense by doing precisely that, searching the Scriptures to prove this out. Here we go! So, let's first go back to the beginning of Creation…

32

To "*Hover*" is a Hebrew word that is used to describe a Momma bird fluttering her wings right above her nest to look after what she had given Birth to, and to care for her young offspring. We see this clearly shown in the Scripture below, directly comparing this nurturing behavior to the LORD GOD.

*Deuteronomy 32:11-12*
**In the same way that an Eagle stirs up its nest and <u>hovers</u> over its young, that spreads its wings to catch them and carries them up higher, so the LORD alone guided them.**

Next, during this same time of Creation, we see GOD (*Elohim*) talking amongst Themselves about creating mankind. You will see that this is an essential dialogue to show us that "*GOD*" is made up of more than one Person, but more importantly, it will show us something much more profound… let's read on.

*Genesis 1:26-28*
*Then **GOD** said, "**Let Us** make mankind in **Our image**, according to **Our likeness**; let them have dominion over the fish of the sea, over the birds of the air, and over the cattle, over all the Earth and over every creeping thing that creeps on the Earth." **So, GOD created man in Their own image; in the image of GOD; male and female GOD created them.** Then GOD blessed them, and GOD said to them, "Be fruitful and multiply; fill the Earth and subdue it; have dominion over the fish of the sea, over the birds of the air, and over every living thing that moves on the Earth."*

This dialogue is truly remarkable to me; it clearly shows us that GOD has both characteristics of male and female gender within the context of the Plural GODHEAD... meaning, the Father, the Son, and the Holy Spirit. So, in this same context, we have a spirit, Soul, and body (three-in-one) and have been created in the Image and Likeness of Them... just as They are... Three-in-One... Male and Female. Pretty powerful, right?

Ok, so let's continue Walking this out. We need to ask ourselves if this is consistent with what we know about GOD in the Old Testament and the New Testament.

So, now let's look specifically at some of the Scriptures regarding the Feminine characteristics of the GODHEAD that seem to show clearly that they are attributes of the Holy Spirit.

# CHAPTER THREE

# THE WORD "SPIRIT"

In the Old Testament, the Holy Spirit was primarily referred to as "*The Spirit of GOD*" or "*The Spirit of the LORD*", but also as The Spirit of Wisdom, Spirit of Life, Spirit of Understanding, Spirit of Counsel, Spirit of Grace and Supplication, Spirit of Might, Spirit of the Knowledge and Reverence of the LORD, or simply stated, "The Spirit". The phrase "*Holy Spirit*", or "*Ruach Ha'Kodesh*" in Hebrew, was only used 3 times in the Old Testament, but this phrase was used 135 times in the New Testament, showing us that the way we interact and understand the GODHEAD was, and is, progressively changing.

In the New Testament, the phrase "*Holy Spirit*" was first introduced to us by the Angel Gabriel to Mary when telling her that she was about to become pregnant carrying Jesus. This appears to be very interesting timing, primarily because this particular event corresponds to the first time the Holy Spirit is mentioned in the New Testament. Jesus and His Apostles and Disciples would continue to primarily refer to "*The Spirit*" by this new term, "*The Holy Spirit*", but at times was also referred to as The Spirit of Truth, Spirit of Holiness, Spirit of the Living GOD, Spirit of Revelation, Spirit of Messiah, Spirit of Glory, Spirit of Grace, Spirit of Promise, Spirit of Adoption, Spirit of Jesus, the Messiah, as well as "*The Spirit*".

The word for "*Spirit*" in the Old Testament Hebrew ( רוּחַ ) "*Ruach*", pronounced "Ru-ak", is actually a "Feminine" word. The word "*Spirit*" in the New Testament Greek ( Πνεῦμα ) "*Pneuma*", pronounced "Nu-ma", is a "Neuter" word. What is also significant to note is that when Jesus spoke, He spoke in either Hebrew or Aramaic, but not Greek. Greek was the primary "Written" language of the day and is what most Scribes would have used when writing down and transcribing what was told to them verbally by Paul and the other Apostles.

The Hebrew and Latin languages were also known written languages of the region; Hebrew was primarily used in Israel by those educated in the Law of Moses, and Latin was also commonly used because of the Roman Empire's rule.

Do you recall what languages were written on the sign that Pontius Pilate had placed on the cross stating that Jesus was the "*King of the Jews*"? (John 19:20)  They were in Hebrew, Greek, and Latin. The reason all of this is significant is that although the word for "*Spirit*" in Greek is Neuter, in both Hebrew and Aramaic, which Jesus spoke, the word for "*Spirit*" is Feminine.

In both the Old and New Testaments, the Holy Spirit is referred to as the Spirit of Wisdom.  The reason this particular Title is so exciting and so relevant to Walking this out, is that "*Wisdom*" is most often referred to as "*Her*" and "*She*" in these various Scriptures. In Hebrew, the word for Wisdom ( חָכְמָה ) pronounced "Chok-mah", is a Noun, but most importantly, it is also a Feminine word.  Jesus even said in Luke 7:35, "*Wisdom is justified by all Her Children*"

### Proverbs 3:13-26
*Happy is the man who finds **Wisdom**, and the man who gains **Understanding**; for **Her** proceeds are better than the profits of silver, and **Her** gain than fine gold.  **She** is more precious than rubies, and all the things you may desire cannot compare with **Her**.  Length of days is in **Her** right-hand, in **Her** left-hand riches and honor.  **Her** ways are ways of pleasantness, and all **Her** paths are Peace.  **She is a Tree of Life** to those who take hold of **Her**, and happy are all who hold on to **Her**.*

*The LORD **by Wisdom** founded the Earth; by
Understanding established the Heavens; by Knowledge
the depths were broken up, and clouds drop down the
dew. My son, let them not depart from your eyes – keep
sound Wisdom and discretion; so they will be **Life** to your
Soul and **Grace** to your neck. Then you will Walk safely in
your way, and your foot will not stumble. When you lie
down, you will not be afraid; yes, you will lie down and
your sleep will be sweet. Do not be afraid of sudden terror,
nor of trouble from the wicked when it comes; for the LORD
will be your confidence, and will keep your foot from being
caught.*

Going back to what you read earlier, that the Holy Spirit is referred to as the Spirit of Wisdom, the Spirit of Understanding, the Spirit of the Knowledge, the Spirit of Life, and the Spirit of Grace. Interestingly enough, this is a direct reference to how the LORD created the Heavens and the Earth as we just read in Proverbs 3 above. This also mirrors the Creation account as shown in Genesis 1 below, where the Spirit of GOD was intimately involved in creating the Heavens and the Earth and was Hovering over it. Both of these Scriptures are clearly showing us that the same "One" was active in Creation, demonstrating to us that "*Wisdom*" and "*The Spirit of GOD*" are One and the same Person.

*Genesis 1:1-2*
*In the beginning, **GOD created the Heavens and the Earth**.
Now the Earth was formless and empty, darkness was over
the surface of the deep, and the **Spirit of GOD** was **hovering**
over the waters.*

Ok, so let's continue to Walk this out…

# CHAPTER FOUR

# OUR NEW BIRTH

It is pretty common for us to just skim over the Scriptures stating we must be Born-Again without much more thought than contemplating the new person we are in Christ Jesus, now that we are Believers. Although that is true, I would like us to dig a little deeper into this subject, and not just stay on the surface.

Women – specifically, Females – give Birth. This is true for most animals on Earth as well. It is a universal norm that GOD placed into the fabric of all of Creation that Females give Birth. This Scripture in John 3 clearly shows us the parallel between the Birth of our Flesh in water from a woman, and our new Birth from The Spirit, of our new spirit. Our new Birth is by and through the Holy Spirit. This Scripture clearly indicates the parallel of the Holy Spirit giving Birth to our new spirit, and directly comparing it to a woman giving Birth to our Flesh – which is *absolutely* something that males do not do. This topic was so significant to GOD that Jesus Himself stated it so profoundly! Therefore, it must be given the attention it deserves.

Now let's read John 3 again, keeping that in mind…

*Jesus answered, "Most assuredly, I say to you, unless one is born of water **and** The Spirit, you cannot enter the Kingdom of GOD. That which is **born of the Flesh** is flesh, and that which is **born of The Spirit** is spirit.*

This shows us that we cannot enter the Kingdom of GOD unless we are born of Flesh by a woman *and* that our new spirit must be Born of the Holy Spirit. The water mentioned in Scripture is the water that comes out when the "Water Breaks", which most women understand perfectly.

Paul the Apostle expresses this in another way, but seems to communicate the same thing when he directly equates the Birth of a woman with our new Birth by the Holy Spirit.

*Galatians 4:28-31*
*Now you, brothers and sisters, like Isaac was, are Children of Promise. But, just as then, he who was **born according to the Flesh** persecuted him who was **born according to The Spirit**, so it is the same now. However, what does the Scripture say? "Cast out the slave woman and her son, for the son **of the slave woman** shall not share in the inheritance with the son **of the Free Woman**." So then, **brothers and sisters, we are** not children of the slave woman, but **of the Free Woman**.*

Paul equates being *"Born of the Flesh"* to a *"slave woman"*, since our Flesh is a slave to sin, then equates being *"Born of the Spirit"* to a *"Free Woman"*. Paul says it another way in 2 Corinthians 3:17, *"where the Spirit of the LORD is, there is Freedom."*

Here are some additional Scriptures showing that it is The Holy Spirit that gives Life to our spirit. There are also references to how The Spirit is the "*Breath of Life*", and Jesus reflects that when He "*breathes*" on the Apostles for them to be Born-Again. This event occurred *before* the Holy Spirit was poured out at Pentecost, when they all received Powers and Gifts. We see that it is through this process that we become sons and daughters of GOD, and therefore, heirs that can approach GOD as a Child of GOD.

### *John 20:21-22*
*So Jesus said to the Apostles, "Peace to you! As the Father has sent Me, I also send you." And when He had said this, **He breathed on them, and said, "Receive the Holy Spirit.**"* (At this time, Jesus had not yet returned to Heaven, so the Holy Spirit had not been sent by the Father into the world for them to be Born-Again - see John 16:7)

### *John 16:7*
Jesus speaking: *"Nevertheless, I tell you the truth. It is to your advantage that I go away; for **if I do not go away, the Comforter will not come to you; but if I depart, I will send Her to you.**"*

### *John 6:63-65*
Jesus speaking: *"**It is The Spirit who gives Life**; the Flesh profits nothing. **The words that I speak to you are Spirit, and they are Life.** But, there are some of you who do not believe." For Jesus knew from the beginning who they were who did not believe, and who would betray Him. And He said, "Therefore, I have said to you that no one can come to Me unless it has been granted to him by My Father."*

*John 3:5-8*

*Jesus answered, "Most assuredly, I say to you, **unless one is born of water and The Spirit, you cannot enter the Kingdom of GOD**. That which is born of the Flesh is flesh, and **that which is born of The Spirit is spirit**. Do not marvel that I said to you, 'You must be Born-Again.' **The <u>wind blows where it wishes</u>**, and you hear the sound of it, but cannot tell where it comes from and where it goes. **So is everyone who is born of The Spirit."**

*Galatians 4:1-7*

*Now I say, that as long as the heir is a child, he does not differ at all from a slave, though he is master of all, but is under guardians and stewards until the time appointed by the father. Even so we, when we were children, were held in bondage under the basic principles of the world. But when the fullness of the time had come, GOD sent forth His Son, born of a woman, born under the Law, to redeem those who were under the Law, **that we might receive the <u>adoption as both sons and daughters, and heirs</u>. And because you are sons, GOD has sent forth The Spirit of His Son into your hearts, crying out, "Abba, Father!"*** ("Daddy, Father!") ***Therefore, <u>you are no longer a slave but a son, and if a son, then also an heir through GOD</u>.***

In the Old Testament, throughout the Book of Psalms, you see the word "*Selah*" that David used at the end of many Verses in these Psalms. It means to "Pause and reflect on what you just read or heard." I feel this is one of those moments.

SELAH...

# CHAPTER FIVE

# ASSUMPTIONS WERE MADE

Do you remember earlier when I stated that "Our Traditions can interfere with GOD's Truth"? Well, I would like you to keep that in mind now.

Jesus told us directly that that Holy Spirit lives inside us as Believers, and does not live inside the Unbelievers of the world. This concept is written about in John 14. So, I want to use these two Verses to illustrate something that became clear to me when I first Walked out this Revelation.

*John 14:16-17*
Jesus speaking: *"And I will ask the Father, and another **Comforter** will be given to you, that will stay with you forever – **the Spirit of Truth**, whom the world is not able to receive, because it neither sees **Her**, nor knows **Her**; but you know **Her**, for **She** resides with you, and will be in you."*

Now, I know most of you reading this just thought, "What? Hold on, I never read that before!" Well... you would be correct. You see, I have noticed that throughout the many different Bible Translations available, that the Translators, as well-intentioned as they may have been, made "Assumptions" and either added Pronouns that were not in the original text, or made an assumption and just "chose one".

The following is John 14:16-17 in the original Greek text:

**16** Κἀγὼ ἐρωτήσω τὸν Πατέρα καὶ ἄλλον Παράκλητον δώσει ὑμῖν ἵνα ᾖ μεθ' ὑμῶν εἰς τὸν αἰῶνα, **17** τὸ Πνεῦμα τῆς ἀληθείας, ὃ ὁ κόσμος οὐ δύναται λαβεῖν, ὅτι οὐ θεωρεῖ **αὐτὸ** οὐδὲ γινώσκει ὑμεῖς γινώσκετε **αὐτό**, ὅτι παρ' ὑμῖν μένει καὶ ἐν ὑμῖν ἔσται.

I know most of us do not read Greek, but let me first draw your attention to the word **αὐτὸ**, used twice in these two Verses here in John 14, pronounced "Afto" and is a Neuter Pronoun, meaning the word is not Masculine or Feminine, and is used when the gender is not known. The proper translation might be "The One" or "This One" or "It", but they _all_ chose the word "He"… thus assigning a male gender to the Holy Spirit. This Greek word can certainly mean "He or Him" _if_ the topic is about a male, or "She or Her" _if_ the topic is about a female, but what I am conveying is that they made a choice.

A very interesting point to note is that there are in fact, specific Greek words for the Pronouns "Him" and for "Her", but those words were not used here. The Greek word **αὐτός** which is a Masculine Pronoun, pronounced "Aftos", means "He or Him" and is used when the topic is known to be about a male. The Greek word **αὐτή** which is a Feminine Pronoun, pronounced "Afti", means "She or Her" and is used when the topic is known to be about a female.

What I find very interesting is that the Translators made a choice, and just chose a gender. I can't say I fully understand, nor do I agree with their choice, but it is a choice, nonetheless. They seem to have made a huge assumption about the Topic of the gender of the Holy Spirit, and regarding the Feminine vs Masculine attributes.

That assumption appears to contradict most Scriptures about the clearly Feminine attributes and characteristics of The Spirit. Now I realize that in the English language, Pronouns are sometimes added for continuity of the translated sentence, as I even did when I added the Pronouns "Her" and "She" to the sentence, but I am primarily focusing on the "Assumption" of *choosing a gender*.

Ok, so just in case any of you are interested in doing a deep dive into the Greek words used in these sentences, to see what the Translation really says, you can see many details about each of the Greek words used in John 14:16-17 shown in the Table below.

| 2504 [e]<br>Kagō<br>Κἀγὼ<br>And I<br>PPro-N1S | 2065 [e]<br>erōtēsō<br>ἐρωτήσω<br>will ask<br>V-FIA-1S | 3588 [e]<br>ton<br>τὸν<br>the<br>Art-AMS | 3962 [e]<br>Patera<br>Πατέρα<br>Father,<br>N-AMS | 2532 [e]<br>kai<br>καὶ<br>and<br>Conj | 243 [e]<br>allon<br>ἄλλον<br>another<br>Adj-AMS | 3875 [e]<br>Paraklēton<br>Παράκλητον<br>Helper (Comforter)<br>N-AMS | | |
|---|---|---|---|---|---|---|---|---|
| 1325 [e]<br>dōsei<br>δώσει<br>be given<br>V-FIA-3S | 4771 [e]<br>hymin<br>ὑμῖν<br>you,<br>PPro-D2P | 2443 [e]<br>hina<br>ἵνα<br>so that<br>Conj | 1510 [e]<br>ē<br>ἦ<br>to be<br>V-PSA-3S | 3326 [e]<br>meth'<br>«μεθ'<br>with<br>Prep | 4771 [e]<br>hymōn<br>ὑμῶν<br>you<br>PPro-G2P | 1519 [e]<br>eis<br>εἰς<br>to<br>Prep | 3588 [e]<br>ton<br>τὸν<br>the<br>Art-AMS | 165 [e]<br>aiōna<br>αἰῶνα»<br>age –<br>N-AMS |
| 3588 [e]<br>to<br>τὸ<br>the<br>Art-ANS | 4151 [e]<br>Pneuma<br>Πνεῦμα<br>Spirit<br>N-ANS | 3588 [e]<br>tēs<br>τῆς<br>of the<br>Art-GFS | 225 [e]<br>alētheias<br>ἀληθείας<br>truth,<br>N-GFS | 3739 [e]<br>ho<br>ὃ<br>whom<br>RelPro-ANS | 3588 [e]<br>ho<br>ὁ<br>the<br>Art-NMS | 2889 [e]<br>kosmos<br>κόσμος<br>world<br>N-NMS | 3756 [e]<br>ou<br>οὐ<br>not<br>Adv | |
| 1410 [e]<br>dynatai<br>δύναται<br>able<br>V-PIM/P-3S | 2983 [e]<br>labein<br>λαβεῖν<br>to receive,<br>V-ANA | 3754 [e]<br>hoti<br>ὅτι<br>because<br>Conj | 3756 [e]<br>ou<br>οὐ<br>not<br>Adv | 2334 [e]<br>theōrei<br>θεωρεῖ<br>does see<br>V-PIA-3S | 846 [e]<br>auto<br>αὐτὸ<br>Her (Him, She, He),<br>PPro-AN3S | | 3761 [e]<br>oude<br>οὐδὲ<br>nor<br>Conj | |
| 1097 [e]<br>ginōskei<br>γινώσκει<br>know.<br>V-PIA-3S | 4771 [e]<br>hymeis<br>ὑμεῖς<br>But you<br>PPro-N2P | 1097 [e]<br>ginōskete<br>γινώσκετε<br>know<br>V-PIA-2P | 846 [e]<br>auto<br>αὐτὸ<br>Her (Him, She, He),<br>PPro-AN3S | | | 3754 [e]<br>hoti<br>ὅτι<br>for<br>Conj | 3844 [e]<br>par'<br>παρ'<br>with<br>Prep | |
| 4771 [e]<br>hymin<br>ὑμῖν<br>you<br>PPro-D2P | 3306 [e]<br>menei<br>μένει<br>resides,<br>V-PIA-3S | 2532 [e]<br>kai<br>καὶ<br>and<br>Conj | 1722 [e]<br>en<br>ἐν<br>in<br>Prep | 4771 [e]<br>hymin<br>ὑμῖν<br>you<br>PPro-D2P | 1510 [e]<br>estai<br>ἔσται<br>will be.<br>V-FIM-3S | | | |

I would like to illustrate another aspect of the Translator's choices, which would be the number of _Added Pronouns_ within each Translation. In the following examples of Scripture, if the word was one of the two original Greek words, **αὐτὸ**, then I underlined it in **Blue**. If it was added for English continuity by the Translator, then I just highlighted it in **Red**. As a reminder, let's look again at how I translated these Verses myself from the original Greek:

### John 14:16-17
_"And I will ask the Father, and another Comforter will be given to you, that will stay with you forever – the Spirit of Truth, whom the world is not able to receive, because it neither sees Her, nor knows Her; but you know Her, for She resides with you, and will be in you."_

As you will see by the next five different Translations, the content is the same, but the number of "Added Pronouns" (again in Red) are vastly different, and they all made the same Assumption about gender. But, the question is…Why? Go ahead and read all five versions and see what differences you can find.

### John 14:16-17
_**16** And I will pray the Father, and He will give you another Helper, that He may abide with you forever— **17** the Spirit of truth, whom the world cannot receive, because it neither sees Him nor knows Him; but you know Him, for He dwells with you and will be in you._
_**(New King James Version - NKJV)**_

48

*John 14:16-17*

*16 And I will ask the Father, and **he** will give you another advocate to help you and be with you forever— 17 the Spirit of truth. The world cannot accept **him**, because it neither sees **him** nor knows **him**. But you know **him**, for **he** lives with you and will be in you.*
**(New International Version - NIV)**


*John 14:16-17*

*16 I will ask the Father, and **he** will give you another Helper to be with you forever. 17 The Helper is the Spirit of truth. The people of the world cannot accept **him**, because they don't see **him** or know **him**. But you know **him**. **He** lives with you, and **he** will be in you.*
**(Easy-to-Read Version - ERV)**


*John 14:16-17*

*16 And I will ask the Father, and **he** will give you another Advocate, who will never leave you. 17 **He** is the Holy Spirit, who leads into all truth. The world cannot receive **him**, because it isn't looking for **him** and doesn't recognize **him**. But you know **him**, because **he** lives with you now and later will be in you.*
**(New Living Translation - NLT)**


*John 14:16-17*

*16 And I will ask the Father, and **he** will give you another Helper, to be with you forever, 17 even the Spirit of truth, whom the world cannot receive, because it neither sees **him** nor knows **him**. You know **him**, for **he** dwells with you and will be in you.*
**(English Standard Version - ESV)**

What became clear to me was that when referring to the Father or the Holy Spirit, the Translators used the same "He" or "Him" Pronouns, even when it wasn't there in the original Greek Text. Also, they all consistently translated the Greek word αὐτὸ to "Him", even though it could be "Her" given the context. That is truly astonishing to me! As you can also see, out of all the Translations I showed you, my Translation added the least number of Pronouns for English continuity, other than those included from the original Greek. I only added **two** Pronouns, whereas all the other Translators added between **three** to **five**. Most of them also made it difficult for the reader to distinguish the difference between a mortal person and Divinity by not capitalizing the Nouns and Pronouns that referred to the Father or the Holy Spirit.

It is worth noting that I chose _only_ to use "Her" or "She", when referring to the Holy Spirit, **if** the word in the original text reflected that same "Neuter Pronoun" that could be used to describe either gender. However, all of the Scriptures I have shared, and will share, referring to "*Wisdom*", had already used the Feminine Pronouns for "Her" or "She" in the original text to describe the Person called "*Wisdom*". I did not change them, which adds weight to support this Revelation. A couple of these unchanged examples were given back on page 37; as shown in Proverbs 3:13-26, and also in Luke 7:35 when Jesus said, "*Wisdom is justified by all _Her_ Children*"

Ok, so let's continue on and see if we can identify the reason why the Translators made their "choice", and hopefully, that it will become more apparent to us, or perhaps, we are left to our own thoughts about their motivations. Either way, let's continue to Walk this out and see which Pronoun that _you would_ end up choosing, given the entirety of the Scriptures referring to who the Holy Spirit truly is.

# CHAPTER SIX

# WHAT REALLY HAPPENED TO MARY?

I want you to try and imagine the following scenario, and see if you get a clearer picture of what really happened to Mary back then. Gabriel, who is a very high-level Angel, had been used by GOD many times in the past to bring messages to Humanity. This time, he was sent to Mary to ask her permission if she would be willing to perform a crucial task for The LORD GOD, which was to bring the Son of GOD into this world, by being a Surrogate Mother. Ok, so let's take a closer look at that Scripture again:

*<u>Luke 1:26-38</u>*
*Now in the sixth month of Elizabeth's pregnancy, **the Angel Gabriel was sent by GOD** to a City of Galilee named Nazareth, **to a Virgin** Engaged to be married to a man whose name was Joseph, and a descendant of King David. **The Virgin's name was Mary.** The Angel went to her and said, "Rejoice, highly favored one, the LORD is with you; blessed are you among women!" Mary was greatly troubled at his words and wondered what kind of greeting this was. Then the Angel said to her, "Do not be afraid Mary, for you have found favor with GOD. And behold, you will conceive in your womb and bring forth a Son, and shall call His name Jesus. He will be great, and will be called the Son of the Highest, and The LORD GOD will give Him the throne of His father David. And He will reign over the house of Jacob forever, and of His Kingdom there will be no end." Then Mary said to the Angel, "How can this be, since I have not been with a man before?" And the Angel answered and said to her, "**The Holy Spirit will come upon you, <u>and</u> the Power of the Most High will overshadow you; therefore, also, that Holy One who is to***

*be born will be called the Son of GOD. Now indeed, Elizabeth, your cousin, has also conceived a son* (John the Baptist) *in her old age; and this is now the sixth month for her who was called barren. For with GOD, nothing will be impossible." Then Mary said, "Behold the maidservant of the LORD! Let it be to me according to your word." And the Angel departed from her.*

Now, as we look at this Scripture, what has become clear to me is that the Holy Spirit occupied the body of Mary first, and then the Father did as well. They are both Spirit, and so in the Spirit, they both joined up together in the womb of Mary, to conceive Their Son Jesus inside her Virgin body. This scenario is wholly consistent with a "*Virgin conceiving*" as it is mentioned Prophetically in Isaiah 7.

*Isaiah 7:14*
*Therefore the Lord* (The Father) *He personally will give you all a sign: Behold, the Virgin shall conceive* (become pregnant, carry in her womb) *and bear a Son, and His name will be called Immanuel.* (God with us)

First of all, allow me to clarify something: There are some large mainstream "Christian" Religions out there that "*suggest*", or will even teach as "*fact*", what most of us would consider a dangerous false doctrine. They teach that either Gabriel, the Father, or the Holy Spirit actually had literal, physical, sexual intercourse with Mary, and that was how she became pregnant. For example, one of them teaches that the Father explicitly came down in bodily form and had literal sex with Mary. This narrative would not only completely destroy the idea of her being a Virgin that conceived miraculously, but instead, would merely be stating that she was a Virgin _before_ she conceived. Many women are in that state when they are first married, and then conceive the first time they are joined with their new husband. This scenario would also make Mary guilty of committing Adultery since she was Engaged to Joseph, and therefore could have been stoned to death based on the Law. Basically, this scenario was precisely what Joseph was worried about, and was also written about in the following Scripture, but the Angel told him clearly that _this was not true_!

### _Matthew 1:18-25_

_Now, this is how the Birth of Jesus, the Messiah, came about: His mother **Mary was Engaged to be married to Joseph**, but before they were intimate, she was found to be carrying in her womb that which belongs to the Holy Spirit. Now Joseph, her husband, was a good man, and did not want to expose her to public disgrace_ (or stoning), _so he had planned to divorce her privately._

_But as he had thought about these things, an Angel of the_ LORD _appeared to him in a Dream and said, "**Joseph, son of David, do not be afraid to take Mary as your wife, because that which is conceived within her is from out of The Spirit and is Holy.** And a Son will be born, and you will call him by the name of Jesus, for He will save His people from their sins. All this took place to fulfill what the_ LORD _had said through the Prophet: 'The Virgin will carry in her womb and give Birth to a Son, and will call His name Immanuel' which means "God with us."_

_Awaking from his sleep, **Joseph** did what the Angel of the_ LORD _had commanded him and **received Mary as his wife**. But **he was not intimate with her until after she gave Birth to a Son**. And he gave Him the name Jesus._

This idea, basically, of Immortals having sex with Mortals, in part, comes from the fact that Angels have actually done this in the past. In Genesis 6:1-7, we can plainly see what happened when this co-mingling of male Angels and female Humans occurred, even though it was absolutely forbidden by GOD. We can then see in the subsequent Chapters in Genesis that this was the primary reason why GOD destroyed the Earth with the flood during Noah's time; because the genetics of the Human Race and the Animals had been corrupted. The Books of Enoch and Jubilees go into this topic in much more detail, but that is another study altogether.

The idea that either Gabriel, the Father, or the Holy Spirit had literal, physical, sexual intercourse with Mary, is also related to this prior forbidden interaction and is the basis for the stories of Zeus, and other "gods", coming down to have sex with Human women. You see, this occurred because the Angels that started co-mingling with women back then, made themselves out to be "gods", and their resulting children out to be "demigods", just as we have read in Greek "Mythology".

These theories about Gabriel, the Father, or the Holy Spirit having sex with Mary have no basis in fact, but are merely speculation and assumptions to help them explain what is easily explainable in the context of the Revelation that I have been sharing with you.

Ok, so now that we dealt with the idea of Mary's virginity, I would like to use the same Scripture to point out a fascinating choice of words that the Holy Spirit gave for Matthew to use when describing the conception of Jesus within Mary. I will elaborate, but first, let's re-read these Verses, but this time, pay very close attention to the words in the three phrases I have highlighted. This choice of words will become more apparent in a moment.

### Matthew 1:18-25

*Now, this is how the Birth of Jesus, the Messiah, came about: His mother Mary was Engaged to be married to Joseph, but before they were intimate, she was found to be **carrying in her womb that which belongs to the Holy Spirit**. Now Joseph, her husband, was a good man, and did not want to expose her to public disgrace* (or stoning), *so he had planned to divorce her privately.*

*But as he had thought about these things, an Angel of the LORD appeared to him in a Dream and said, "Joseph, son of David, do not be afraid to take Mary as your wife, because **that which is conceived within her is from out of The Spirit and is Holy**. And a Son will be born, and you will call Him by the name of Jesus, for He will save His people from their sins. All this took place to fulfill what the LORD had said through the Prophet: 'The Virgin will carry in her womb and give Birth to a Son, and will call His name Immanuel' which means "God with us."*

*Awaking from his sleep, Joseph did what the Angel of the LORD had commanded him and received Mary as his wife. But he was not intimate with her until after she gave Birth to a Son. And he gave Him the name Jesus.*

The words that I highlighted in the previous Verses, when read in the original Greek and Hebrew, provide a very interesting picture. The **first phrase**, *"carrying in her womb that which belongs to the Holy Spirit"* provides a clear picture of the idea of being a "Surrogate Mother", meaning that the Baby was not Mary's Baby; she was only "Carrying" it. This is further reinforced at the end of this phrase by the statement that the Baby *"belongs to the Holy Spirit"*, and therefore does not belong to Mary.

In the **second phrase**, *"that which is conceived within her is from out of The Spirit and is Holy"* shows us that the Baby conceived within her was actually *"from out of The Spirit"*, meaning not only was it *"from"* the Holy Spirit, but it was also *"out of"* the Holy Spirit. Combining these two ideas means that this Baby did not belong to Mary because the Egg did not come *"from out of"* Mary, but *"from out of"* the Holy Spirit, and that the conception was indeed Holy, as it would need to be for Jesus to be without sin.

Humanity is sinful because we are all under the Curse of Adam & Eve, so, therefore, the Human Egg, in our "fallen state", would _not_ be called *"Holy"* from the perspective of the "Sinful Nature" that we all are subjected to. If Mary's Egg were part of the conception, and the Holy Spirit was the "male side", as most people tell each other, then Jesus would _not_ be *"Holy"* and without Sin… He would have been created with a sinful "component", meaning the Egg from Mary. Additionally, the only way for the conception to be Holy would be if the Egg came from the Holy Spirit, and for the seed to come from the Father. Here are a couple of Verses that support this concept.

*Matthew 7:18*
**"A bad tree cannot produce good fruit."**

## John 3:6
*"That which is born of the Flesh is flesh, and that which is born of the Spirit is spirit."*

Another Verse appears to be related to this topic, but it never made sense to me until after I Walked out this Revelation. It is in Genesis 3:15 and is supported by Scriptures in the New Testament. The phrase that never made sense to me before is: *"her Seed"*.

Seed is usually used to describe the male semen. This is the only place in the Bible that this Hebrew phrase was used, and is Translated to mean *"her Seed"*. In the New Testament, it clearly was shown to mean this reference was about Jesus. I believe it is because the idea of Surrogacy would be described similarly back then. If a fertilized Egg is planted in the Uterus of a woman to grow, would that not be equated to how you would plant a "seed" in soil? Let's look at these Scriptures and see if this idea becomes clearer.

## Genesis 3:15
The LORD GOD speaking: *"I will cause hostility between you* (Satan) *and the woman, and also between your seed and **her Seed**; He* (Jesus) *shall bruise your head, and you shall bruise His heel."*

## Galatians 3:16,19
*Now to Abraham and **his Seed** were the promises made. He does not say, "And to seeds," as of many people, but as of one, "And to your **Seed**," who is* (Jesus) ***the Messiah**. What purpose then does the law serve? It was added because of transgressions, till **the Seed** should come to whom the promise was made*

Finally, in the **third phrase**, *"The Virgin will carry in her womb"*, is a quote originally from the Old Testament Book of Isaiah, in Hebrew, regarding the Virgin Birth. What I find interesting is that even though many translations render this incorrectly, the original Old Testament Hebrew and the New Testament Greek phrase's emphasis is on the fact that the Prophesied Virgin will *"carry in her womb"* the Son who will be called *"God with us"*. This, yet again, is a very interesting choice of words, in both languages, that seems to reinforce the idea of Surrogacy.

Now, let's go over this from a more "Eternal Perspective":

1. Jesus is the Son of GOD, who existed, before the Creation of the world, with His Parents, the Father, and the Holy Spirit.

*John 1:1,14*
***In the beginning,*** *was the Word, and the Word was **with GOD**, and the Word **was God** And the Word **became flesh** and dwelt among us, and we beheld His Glory, the Glory as of **the One and only offspring** of the Father, full of Grace and Truth.*

*John 17:5,24*
Jesus speaking: *"Father, Glorify Me together alongside You, with the **Glory which I had with You before the world began**. Father, I want those You have given Me to be with Me where I am, and to see My Glory, the Glory You have given Me because **You loved Me before the Creation of the world**."*

2. The Father and the Holy Spirit formed a "sinless Body"; a Body made completely from Them; made for Their Son to dwell in while among us on Earth, as well as the Body that Jesus could sacrifice as the perfect Lamb of GOD.

*Colossians 2:9*
*For **in Jesus dwells all the completeness of the GODHEAD in bodily form**.* (Not ½ GOD, ½ Mary)

*Hebrews 10:5*
*Therefore, **when Jesus came into the world, He said to the Father**: "Animal sacrifice and offering You did not desire, but **a Body that You have prepared for Me**."*

*Colossians 1:15*
**The Son is the image of the invisible GOD, the Firstborn over all Creation.**

3. Jesus then stepped out of Eternity and into the Body that was prepared for Him. He brought His Spirit and His Soul and entered the Body that His Parents created in Mary.

*1 Corinthians 15:47*
*Adam, the first man, was made from the dust of the Earth, while **Christ Jesus, the second man, came from Heaven**.* (Adam was formed by GOD, then his spirit entered after.)

*Hebrews 10:5*
*Therefore, when **Jesus came into** the world, He said to the Father: "Animal sacrifice and offering You did not desire, but **a Body that You have prepared for Me**."*

This concept of Surrogacy is also shown with these Scriptures referencing that Jesus is our Eternal High Priest in the same way as Melchizedek. Most people will focus on His Priestly role and how Jesus intercedes for us forever, similarly to how the High Priest would offer sacrifices for the people. One of the things most people miss is the reference to not having Biological Parents, nor having a Bloodline at all. This perspective is entirely consistent with a Divinely Created Surrogate Pregnancy.

### *Psalm 110:1-4*

*The LORD says to my Lord* (later shown to be Jesus): *"Sit at My right-hand until I make Your enemies a footstool for Your feet." The LORD will extend Your mighty scepter from Zion, saying, "Rule in the midst of Your enemies!" Your troops will be willing on Your Day of battle. Arrayed in holy splendor, Your young men will come to You like dew from the morning's womb. The LORD has sworn and will not change His mind: "You* (Jesus) *are a priest forever, after the order of Melchizedek."*

### *Acts 2:34-36*

Peter speaking: *For David did not ascend to heaven, and yet he said, "The LORD said to my Lord: 'Sit at My right-hand until I make Your enemies a footstool for Your feet.' " Therefore let all Israel be assured of this: GOD has made this Jesus, whom you crucified, both Lord and Messiah.*

### *Hebrews 7:1-3, 22-25*

*For this Melchizedek, King of Salem, priest of the Most High God, who met Abraham returning from the battle of the kings and blessed him, to whom also Abraham gave a tenth part of all, first being translated "King of*

*Righteousness" and then also King of Salem, meaning "King of Peace",* __*without father,*__ __*without mother,*__ __*without genealogy, having neither beginning of days, nor end of life, but made like the Son of GOD,*__ *remains a priest continually. Because of this oath, Jesus is the one who guarantees this better covenant with GOD. There were many priests under the old system, for death prevented them from remaining in office. But* **because Jesus lives forever, His priesthood lasts forever.** *Therefore, He is able, once and forever, to save completely those who come to GOD through Him.* **He lives forever to intercede with GOD on their behalf.**

Wow! This is clearly stating that Jesus, the Son of GOD, just like Melchizedek, did not have either conventional Human parents or a Human genetic bloodline. Additionally, this reinforces the fact that Jesus was Eternal before His Birth, in that He had *"neither beginning of days, nor end of life"* If Mary actually was the mother of Jesus, using her own Egg, then these Scriptures would not have been able to make these statements so profoundly.

*SELAH...*

# CHAPTER SEVEN

# HOW SHOULD WE REFER TO MARY?

Should we admire Mary for what she did and consider her to have been incredibly blessed? Absolutely! What the LORD GOD did with her was incredible! But, unfortunately, some Religions have not only decided to admire and respect Mary for what she did, by agreeing to bring Jesus the Son of GOD into the world, but have transitioned over to the point of "worshipping" her. I honestly cannot understand this, because it contradicts not only what GOD has stated so profoundly in the Old Testament, but also what is stated in the New Testament as well. What is clear is that we are not supposed to pray to anyone else, or anything else, other than to the Father, in the name of the Son Jesus, and with the Power and Guidance of the Holy Spirit. Jesus gave us a very famous "Model Prayer", where He starts by saying, "*Our Father in Heaven…*", reinforcing this concept. Here are just a few of the numerous Scriptures stating how GOD feels about us worshipping anything, or anyone, that GOD has created, or making Idols of the same, and just how serious that is to GOD.

*1 Timothy 2:5-6*
Paul writing to Timothy: ***For there is One GOD and <u>One Mediator between GOD and mankind, the Man, Christ Jesus</u>, who gave Himself a ransom for all people.*** *This message was given to us at just the right time.*

*Romans 8:26-28*
*Likewise,* ***The Spirit also helps us in our weaknesses***, *for we do not know what we should pray for as we need to, but* ***The Spirit Herself intercedes on our behalf***, *crying out with words that cannot be expressed. Now searching the*

*deepest parts of our hearts, **the purpose of The Spirit is known, because the intercession made by The Spirit for Believers is according to the Will of GOD.** And we know that all things work together for good to those who love GOD, to those who are the Called, according to the divine purpose.*

GOD has made something extremely clear to us, in that we need to make certain that we do not worship anyone or anything else but GOD. Here are several Scriptures that will help you understand just how serious this is to GOD.

*Exodus 20:1-6*
***And GOD spoke** all these words, saying:*

*"I am the LORD your GOD, who brought you out of the land of Egypt, out of the house of bondage.*

***You shall have no other gods before Me!***

***You must not make for yourself a carved image** – any likeness of anything that is in Heaven above, or that is on the Earth beneath, or that is in the Sea; **you must not bow down to them nor worship them.** For I, the LORD your GOD, am a jealous God, who will not tolerate your affection for any other gods. I lay the sins of the parents upon their children; the entire family is affected, even children in the third and fourth generations of those who reject me. But I lavish My unfailing Love and Mercy for a thousand generations on those who love Me and obey My Commands."*

*Leviticus 19:1,4*
*And the LORD spoke to Moses, saying, "**Do not worship Idols!** Do not make statues of gods for yourselves. I am the LORD your GOD!"*

*1 Samuel 12:20-21*

*Samuel answered, "Don't be afraid. It is true that you did all these bad things, but don't stop following the LORD. Serve the LORD with all your heart.* <u>*Idols are only statues – they can't help you! So, don't worship them. Idols can't help you or save you. They are nothing!*</u>*"*

*1 Kings 16:26*

**They worshiped worthless Idols, and <u>this made the LORD GOD of Israel, very angry.</u>**

*2 Kings 17:15-16*

**They rejected the LORD's rules and the covenant He had made with their ancestors and the laws He had warned them to keep. <u>They followed worthless Idols and themselves became worthless.</u> They imitated the Nations around them, although the LORD had ordered them, "Do not do as they do." They forsook all the Commands of the LORD their GOD and made for themselves Idols.**

*Isaiah 44:6-23*

**"Thus says the LORD, the King of Israel, and His** *Redeemer, the LORD of hosts: 'I am the First, and I am the Last;* **besides Me there is no God.** *And who can proclaim as I do? Then let him declare it and set it in order for Me, since I established My ancient people. And the things that are coming and shall come, let them show these to them. Do not fear, nor be afraid; have I not told you from that time, and declared it? You are My witnesses.* **Is there a God besides Me? Indeed, there is no other Rock; I know not one."**

*"Those who make an image, all of them are useless, and their precious things shall not profit; they are their own witnesses; they neither see nor know, that they may be ashamed. Who would form a god or mold an image that profits him nothing? Surely all his companions would be ashamed, and the workmen, they are mere men. Let them all be gathered together, let them stand up; yet they shall fear, they shall be ashamed together. The blacksmith with the tongs works one in the coals, fashions it with hammers, and works it with the strength of his arms. Even so, he is hungry, and his strength fails; he drinks no water and is faint. The craftsman stretches out his rule, he marks one out with chalk; he fashions it with a plane, he marks it out with the compass, and makes it like the figure of a man, according to the beauty of a man, that it may remain in the house. He cuts down cedars for himself, and takes the cypress and the oak; he secures it for himself among the trees of the forest. He plants a pine, and the rain nourishes it. Then it shall be for a man to burn, for he will take some of it and warm himself; yes, he kindles it and bakes bread; indeed, he makes a god and worships it; he makes it a carved image, and falls down to it. He burns half of it in the fire; with this half he eats meat; he roasts a roast, and is satisfied. He even warms himself and says, "Ah! I am warm, I have seen the fire." And the rest of it he makes into a god, his carved image. He falls down before it and worships it, prays to it and says, "Deliver me, for you are my god!" They do not know nor understand; for He has shut their eyes, so that they cannot see, and their hearts, so that they cannot understand. And no one considers in his heart, nor is there knowledge nor understanding to say, "I have burned half of it in the fire, yes, I have also baked bread on its coals; I have roasted meat and eaten it; and shall I make the rest of it an abomination? Shall I fall down before a block of wood?" He feeds on ashes; a deceived heart has turned him aside, and he cannot deliver his Soul, nor say, "Is there not a lie in my right-hand?" "*

*"Remember these, O Jacob, and Israel, for you are My servant; I have formed you, you are My servant; O Israel, you will not be forgotten by Me! I have blotted out, like a thick cloud, your transgressions, and like a cloud, your sins.* **Return to Me, for I have redeemed you.'** *"*


*Jeremiah 10:1-16*

*Hear what the* L*ORD* *says to you, people of Israel.* **This is what the** L*ORD* **says: "Do not learn the ways of the Nations or be terrified by Signs in the Heavens, though the** *Nations are terrified by them.* **For the practices of the peoples are worthless;** *they cut a tree out of the forest, and a craftsman shapes it with his chisel. They adorn it with silver and gold; they fasten it with hammer and nails so it will not totter. Like a scarecrow in a cucumber field,* **their Idols cannot speak; they must be carried around because they cannot walk. Do not fear them; they can do no harm, nor can they do any good.** *"*

**No one is like You,** L**ORD***;* **You are great, and Your Name is mighty in Power.** *Who should not fear You, King of the Nations? This is Your due. Among all the wise leaders of the Nations and in all their kingdoms, there is no one like You.* **They are all senseless and foolish; they are taught by worthless wooden Idols.** *Hammered silver is brought from Tarshish and gold from Uphaz. What the craftsman and goldsmith have made is then dressed in blue and purple –* **all made by skilled workers.** *But* **the** L**ORD is the True G***OD**; the living G*OD*, the eternal King. When angry, the Earth trembles; the Nations cannot endure His wrath. Tell them this: 'These gods, who did not make the Heavens and the Earth, will perish from the Earth and from under the Heavens.' But G*OD* made the Earth by Power, founded the world by Wisdom, and stretched out the Heavens by Understanding. When He thunders, the waters in the*

*Heavens roar; makes clouds rise from the ends of the Earth. He sends lightning with the rain and brings out the wind from His storehouses. Everyone is senseless and without knowledge;* **every goldsmith is shamed by his Idols. The images he makes are a fraud; they have no breath in them. They are worthless, the objects of mockery; when their judgment comes, they will perish.** *He who is the Portion of Jacob is not like these, for He is the Maker of all things, including Israel, the people of His inheritance –* **the LORD Almighty is His Name.**

## Matthew 4:10

*Then* **Jesus said** *to him,* **"Away with you, Satan! For it is written, 'You shall worship the LORD your GOD, and the LORD only shall you serve.' "**

## Mark 12:28-31

*Then one of the scribes came, and having heard them reasoning together, seeing that Jesus had answered them well, tried Testing Him with this question, "Which is the greatest Commandment of all?"* **Jesus answered** *him,* **"The first of all the Commandments is: 'Hear, O Israel, the LORD our GOD, the LORD is One. And you shall love the LORD your GOD with all your heart, with all your Soul, with all your mind, and with all your strength.' This is the first and greatest Commandment.** *And the second, like it, is this: 'You shall love your neighbor as yourself.'* **There is no other Commandment greater than** *these."*

*Revelation 14:6-7*

*Then I saw another Angel flying high in the air, having the everlasting Gospel to preach to those who dwell on the Earth – to every Nation, Tribe, Language, and People – saying with a loud voice, "Fear GOD and give glory to Him, for the hour of His judgment has come. <u>Worship GOD alone</u>, who made Heaven and Earth, the sea and springs of water."*

*Revelation 19:10*

*At this, I fell at the Angel's feet to worship him. But he said to me, "<u>Don't do that!</u> I am a fellow servant like you, and with your brothers and sisters who hold to the testimony of Jesus. <u>Worship GOD!</u> For it is the Spirit of Prophecy who bears testimony to Jesus."*

*Revelation 22:8-9*

*I, John, am the one who heard and saw these things. And when I had heard and seen them, I fell down to worship at the feet of the Angel who had been showing them to me. But he said to me, "<u>Don't do that!</u> I am a fellow servant with you and with your fellow Prophets and with all who keep the words of this scroll. <u>Worship GOD!</u>"*

*1 Corinthians 10:19-22*

*So, am I saying that food sacrificed to an Idol is anything, or that an Idol is anything? No, because <u>an Idol is nothing, and the things offered to Idols are worth nothing.</u> But I am saying that <u>when food</u> (or money, or requests) <u>is sacrificed to Idols, it is an offering to Demons, not to GOD,</u> and I don't want you to share anything with Demons. You cannot drink the cup of the LORD and then*

*go drink a cup that honors Demons too. You cannot share
a meal at the LORD's table and then go share a meal that
honors Demons.* **__Doing that would make the LORD
jealous.__** *Do you really want to do that? Do you think we
are stronger than the LORD is?*

*Acts 10:25-26*
*When Peter entered the house, Cornelius met him. He fell
down at Peter's feet and worshiped him.* **But Peter made
him get up saying, "Stand up! I am only a man like you."**

So, do you remember earlier when we were going over the Chapter on the GODHEAD? I told you that a Term was missing from the descriptions of the Heavenly Monarchy in the Bible… well, that term was "Queen". The Holy Spirit is the Queen! The Father is the King, and Jesus is the Prince.

I firmly believe that if we have a "misconception" of Who the GODHEAD is comprised of – meaning the GODHEAD is made up of three "Males" – this will only serve to encourage "Mary worship" because she then becomes the *"Queen of the Universe"* since people then, in turn, will believe that there are no other females within the Monarchy of the Kingdom of GOD.

All of those many, many Scriptures make it abundantly clear that we should never worship Idols. The warnings are quite clear! Which means… Do Not Worship Mary, Saints, or any other "gods"!

Something to make you truly pause and think about…

# CHAPTER EIGHT

# WHY DOES THIS STILL CONTINUE TODAY?

The Scriptures plainly show us that we are _absolutely never_ to worship Idols, nor ever make Offerings to Idols! It is incredible to me that, in spite of all of the knowledge that is so readily available to us, this still happens today, even though GOD has brought Judgement numerous times on Nations and on Individuals for doing just that. To this day, I see it being done in so many households, Shrines, Temples, and Churches. I have been amazed even to find it being done in the homes of my friends and relatives, like statues of Mary, Catholic Saints, Buddha, Hindu, and other "gods" with Offerings of incense, food, money, notes, and other items at their feet. I have always wondered what they were thinking… Do they really believe that this Idol is "GOD", or even a god? But, then I am reminded that Satan and his Demons love to receive worship for themselves, to keep people from worshipping the One true GOD, the Creator of all things – the Heavens and the Earth, and every living thing in it. My heart grieves for them because these people have been blinded through their "Traditions", are just stumbling through this life, and don't seem to understand why their lives are so full of chaos and disorder.

Just as Paul told us in 1 Corinthians 10:19-22 (page 70), they are actually making these Offerings to Demons, not to GOD, and are inviting these Demons into their lives without even realizing it. This will occur most often because they haven't read the Word of GOD for themselves, so they would be able to know just how wrong this is, and how clearly it is stated, and just how angry it makes GOD when people do this type of thing. If they understood, they would never even consider thinking about doing this.

*Matthew 15:1-3,6-9*

*Then the Scribes and Pharisees who were from Jerusalem came to Jesus, saying, "Why do Your Disciples violate the Traditions of the elders?* **Jesus answered** *and said to them, "**Why do you violate the Commandments of GOD because of your Traditions? By doing this, you have made the Words of GOD worthless by your Traditions!** Hypocrites! Very well did Isaiah Prophesy about you, saying:*

*'These people come near to Me with the words of their mouth, and honor Me with their lips, but their heart is far from Me. And **in vain they worship Me**, teaching in its place as doctrines, the commandments of men.' "*

*Mark 7:8-9,13*

Jesus speaking: *"You have stopped following GOD's Commands, preferring instead the man-made rules you received from others."* **Then Jesus said, "You show great skill in avoiding the Commands of GOD so that you can follow your own teachings!** *So, you are teaching that it is not important to do what GOD says. You think it is more important to follow those Traditions you have, which you pass on to others. And you do so many things like that."*

*1 Peter 1:17-19*

*You pray to GOD and call Him Father, but He **will judge everyone the same way – by the things they do and believe.** So, while you are visiting here on Earth, you should live with Reverence and Respect for GOD. **You** know that in the past, the way you were living was **useless. It was a way of life you learned from those who lived before and were passed down to from your forefathers.***

*But you were saved from that way of living. You were bought, but not with things that ruin like gold or silver. **You were bought with the precious Blood of Jesus, the Messiah's death. He was a pure and perfect sacrificial Lamb.***

Traditions can truly be a compelling and driving force behind the things we do, and the things we believe, especially those Traditions that have been handed down through many generations within our families. These Traditions from our families can be a powerful motivation for us to continue walking down the same path, even if deep inside us, we know it is wrong. The problem is that Traditions can take over and become stronger than our belief in GOD, and our efforts to follow what GOD has said to us through The Word of GOD. Those three Scripture Verses we just read are New Testament references that Jesus and Peter spoke, making very clear statements about how GOD feels regarding our following Traditions, rather than following what GOD has actually told us to do.

These Scriptures are worth re-reading until it sinks in just how strongly GOD feels about us worshipping Idols, and placing our Traditions ahead of GOD's Word; instead, we need to truly understand how GOD said that He *"will judge everyone the same way – by the things they do and believe"*.

# CHAPTER NINE

# How Did Jesus Refer To Mary?

When we take a look at the way Jesus spoke to Mary, an interesting dynamic is revealed. He treated her with respect, but He did not refer to her as His mother. That seems unusual, right? If she genuinely was His mother, then why not acknowledge it, so all of us could know for sure? Let us now look at the Scriptures where Jesus spoke to Mary directly, using the light of all the Scriptures you have just read in the previous Chapters, and let's see what these Scriptures tell us about their relationship.

### John 2:3-4
*When the wine was gone, Jesus' mother said to Him, "They have no more wine." **Jesus replied, "Woman, why do you involve me? My time has not yet come."***

### John 19:25-27
*Near the cross of Jesus stood His mother Mary, His mother's sister, Mary the wife of Clopas, and Mary Magdalene. When Jesus saw His mother there, and John the Disciple whom He loved standing nearby, **He said to her, "Woman, here is your son," and to the Disciple,*** (the Apostle John) **"Here is your mother."** *So, from that time on, this Disciple took her into his own home.*

We see that when John wrote about these events, he referred to Mary as Jesus' mother, but then we see that Jesus simply called her "*woman*". This would absolutely, without question, *not* be a typical way that a man would address his mother during this time period, they were taught to be extremely respectful to their mothers. A child would call their mother - "Imma" which is pronounced "Ee-ma" and is a beautiful Hebrew word ( אִמָּא ). So, why would Jesus make this statement to us? If she genuinely was His mother, then why not acknowledge it, so all of us could know for sure?

You see, Jesus knew He would not only be speaking to the people around Him at the time, but He was speaking to all Believers throughout history. He stated this idea clearly in John 17:20, saying, *"I do not ask for these alone, but also for those who believe in Me, through the words of those in Me"*. So, when Jesus was talking, He knew He was not only saying something to the peoples around Him of that time, He knew that all of the things He was saying would be documented and would affect all of us, in all time periods, because we were the people who would hear from other Believers throughout time *"through the words of those in Me"*.

I feel that Jesus actually expressed clearly to us regarding who Mary was to Him, in that she was just a *"woman"* who was used by GOD, but that she was *not* His Mother. Let's look at a couple more examples of this...

*Mark 3:31-35*
*Then Jesus' mother and brothers arrived. Standing outside, they sent someone in to call Jesus. A crowd was sitting around Him, and they told Him, "Your mother and brothers are outside looking for You." **Jesus asked, "Who are My mother and My brothers?" Then He looked at those seated in a circle around Him and said, "Here are My mother and My brothers! Whoever does GOD's Will is My brother and sister and mother."***

*Luke 11:27-28*
*Now it happened, as Jesus was speaking, that a certain woman from the crowd raised her voice and said to Him, "Blessed is the womb that bore You, and the breasts which nursed You!"* **But Jesus said, "No, blessed rather are those who hear the Words of GOD and obey it!"**

You just read two examples of different events where Jesus had an opportunity to show honor to Mary as His mother, but He did not; instead, He deflected that honor away from Mary, and onto Believers... the same Believers who, coincidentally, would soon be carrying His real Mother, the Holy Spirit.

Could it *also* be He did this because He knew that many in the future would worship Mary as divine, consider her to be the Queen of the Universe, or the mediator between GOD and Humanity, and that He wanted to deflect away from that? It seems very clear that people have revered and worshiped Mary for quite some time, even when she should not be. She was an incredibly blessed woman, used by GOD as a Surrogate mother to Jesus, but she was not His Mother. I believe that if Jesus wanted us to revere her or show her a great deal of honor as "His Mother", then He would have addressed her differently and gone along with those statements about Mary.

Let's now look at how Jesus treated Joseph and Mary as a 12-year-old boy. We can see that Luke referred to both of them as His parents, but did Jesus actually know back then that they were not His "real parents"? Even today, we refer to those who love children as their own, as Parents... Step-Parents, Foster-Parents, Grand-Parents, God-Parents, etc. But, that certainly does not make them the child's "Biological Parents". In Luke 2, we see a fascinating interaction.

*Every year his parents, Joseph and Mary, went up to Jerusalem for the Festival of the Passover. When He was twelve years old, they went up to the Festival, according to the custom. After the Festival was over, while His parents were returning home, the boy Jesus stayed behind in Jerusalem, but they were unaware of it. Thinking He was in their company, they traveled on for a day. Then they began looking for Him among their relatives and friends. When they did not find Him, they went back to Jerusalem to look for Him. After three days, they found Him in the Temple courts, sitting among the teachers, listening to them and asking them questions. Everyone who heard Him was amazed at His understanding and His answers.* **When His parents saw Him, they were astonished. His mother said to Him, "Son, why have you treated us like this?** (Because this would have been disrespectful for a child to do this to their parents of that time period.) *Your father and I have been anxiously searching for you." "Why were you searching for Me?" Jesus asked. "Didn't you know I would have to be in My Father's House?" But they did not understand what He was saying to them. Then He went down to Nazareth with them and decided to become submitted to them.* **But His mother continued thinking about all these things in her heart. And Jesus grew in Wisdom and stature, and in favor with GOD and man.**

Around the age of Twelve, most boys start to become more independent as they approach their teenage years, and along with this independence, can often come rebellion and disrespect. This age is also around the "Age of Accountability", when children become self-aware, have a better understanding of sin and of good and evil, and become directly accountable to GOD for their own actions, no longer being covered by their parents. You see this concept played out even to this day in Jewish Children when they go through their "Coming of Age" or "Spiritual Maturity" Ceremonies, called a "Bar-Mitzvah" for a boy, or a "Bat-Mitzvah" for a girl.

Now, according to Luke 2, you will notice that the actions of Jesus were very independent, but there is something here that I think most people simply skim over. You see, He was not only visiting the Temple, but think about this, He was there for _five days_ without an adult in the family taking care of Him. Remember, they journeyed one day out, one day back, and three days looking for Him. Where did He eat and sleep? How was all this paid for? Remember He was only twelve.

When they finally found Him, He made it clear to Joseph and Mary that they should have known that He would be in the Temple because _that was "His Father's House"_. Jesus seemed genuinely surprised they would even question His actions because of Who He was. But then Jesus does something that most "Teens" don't do at that age; He submitted Himself to them anyway, showing us again that He did not sin against those who had the responsibility to care for Him, as a parent... but _not_ as a mother and father.

What I find most interesting about this account is that it's the only story we have about Jesus from the time He was a Toddler of around 2 years old, to the time He started His ministry at the age of approximately 30 years old. That is a lot of time with only one story, so the question is this... _why that story?_ I believe it is so we could understand the relationship regarding who Joseph and Mary really are to Jesus, and who they are not.


Pause, and think about that for a moment...

I also want to share with you another Revelation I had while Walking this out. It happened as I was looking at all the Scriptures related to the Holy Spirit, and was a deeply emotional experience that I would like to share with you. I think you will find it has an interesting contrast to the other story you just read in Luke 2:41-52.

*Luke 3:21-22*
*When all the people were baptized, it came to pass that*
*Jesus also was baptized; **and while He prayed, the Heaven***
***was opened, and the Holy Spirit descended in bodily form,***
***like a dove, upon Him, and then a voice came from***
***Heaven which said, "You are My beloved Son; in You I***
***am well pleased."***

During the time I was first Walking out this Revelation, I happened to come across this Scripture in Luke, and while reading it, I had a very clear Vision. The Vision was of the Holy Spirit coming down out of the open Heaven, in the bodily form of a Woman with wings, giving off a very bright white light, fluttering Her wings in the same manner as a Dove would as it lands. She then landed directly behind Jesus. I recall as I looked intently at Her in the Vision, I saw such a loving smile on Her face as She wrapped Her arms and wings around Him, hugging Him and laying Her head on His shoulder; She then disappeared within Him.

This was such a beautiful expression of love that a Mother would have for Her Son. Next, I heard the Father's audible voice coming from Heaven saying to Jesus, and all those around who could hear, that Jesus was His Son, that He was loved, and that He is very pleased with Him. When the Vision was over, I couldn't contain my tears; I was feeling such a deep sense of Their love and pride that the Holy Spirit allowed me to feel, and it was truly a deeply emotional experience. This was an amazing interaction between Mother, Father, and Son. They clearly seemed to be announcing to the world, and to Their Son, expressing Their love, pride, and approval for Jesus in starting His ministry, as well as empowering Him by receiving the Holy Spirit. Now think about this in contrast to the interaction Jesus had with Mary and Joseph in Jerusalem at the Temple.

Wow! What a difference!

There is another Scripture I would like you to consider in light of this new context. When a child is left alone and in distress, he may cry out for his parents for help. If we look at what happened later in Jesus' life when He was being crucified, and while carrying the sins of the world upon Him. The Father and the Holy Spirit had to leave Their Son since they could not occupy the same space with all that sin, as it says in: Habakkuk 1:13 *"Your eyes, LORD GOD, are too pure to look on evil"*; 2 Corinthians 5:21 *"GOD made Jesus who had no sin, to be sin for us."*; 1 Peter 2:24 *"Jesus Himself bore our sins in His Body on the cross."* Let us now look at what Jesus did when this happened to Him.

*Matthew 27:46*
*And about the ninth hour, Jesus cried out with a loud voice, saying, "Eli, Eli, lama sabachthani?" that is, "My God, My God, why have You abandoned Me?"*

His Father and Mother just left Him because of the sin of the world He was carrying. Just as a child who is left alone and in trouble would call out, "Mommy! Daddy! Why did you leave Me alone?" The Father is God, and the Holy Spirit is God, so this is wholly consistent with the context of what happened, and the Scriptures.

This all may sound unusual compared to what you have heard in the past, but that does not make it any less true.

# CHAPTER TEN

# WHY SO PROTECTIVE?

Did you ever wonder why the blasphemy of the Holy Spirit is considered "The Unpardonable Sin"? I had often thought about this and wondered what could be so bad that Jesus would tell us that any sin, including killing Him, blasphemy against Him, or blasphemy against the Father, could be forgiven, but _not_ sins committed against the Holy Spirit. You may want to ask yourself... _Why?_

_Matthew 12:31-32_
Jesus speaking: *"Therefore I say to you, every sin and blasphemy will be forgiven men, but the blasphemy against The Spirit will not be forgiven men. Anyone who speaks a word against the Son of Man, it will be forgiven him; but <u>whoever speaks against the Holy Spirit, it will not be forgiven him, either in this age or in the age to come</u>."*

_Mark 3:28-30_
Jesus speaking: *"Assuredly, I say to you, all sins will be forgiven the sons of men, and whatever blasphemies they may utter; but <u>he who blasphemes against the Holy Spirit never has forgiveness, but is subject to eternal condemnation</u>"* – because they said, *"He has an unclean spirit."*

Wow! That seems harsh, right? So... Why? Well, there appears to be built into the fabric of who men are, fundamentally, to be protective of women, but especially of our Mothers. I believe that is what Jesus is doing here. I have never heard anyone give another more reasonable explanation as to why Jesus would have said this.

Along these same lines, this would also be considered blasphemy against *the Father's Wife*. Pause and think about *that* for a moment.

Additionally, we see both Peter and Paul reinforced this idea; Peter, when referring to the consequences of Lying to the Holy Spirit, and Paul, referring to the concept of Grieving the Holy Spirit.

### *Acts 5:1-11*

*But a certain man named Ananias, with Sapphira, his wife, sold a possession. And he kept back part of the proceeds, his wife also being aware of it, and brought a certain part and laid it at the Apostles' feet. But **Peter said**, "Ananias, **why has Satan filled your heart to <u>lie to the Holy Spirit</u>** and keep back part of the price of the land for yourself? While you retained it, was it not your own? And after it was sold, was it not in your own control? Why have you conceived this thing in your heart? <u>**You have not lied to men, but to GOD**</u>." **Then Ananias, hearing these words, fell down and died.** So great fear came upon all those who heard these things. And the young men arose and wrapped him up, carried him out, and buried him. Now it was about three hours later when his wife came in, not knowing what had happened. And Peter answered her, "Tell me whether you sold the land for so much?" She said, "Yes, for so much." Then Peter said to her, "How is it that you have agreed together <u>**to Test the Spirit of the LORD**</u>? Look, the feet of those who have buried your husband are at the door, and they will carry you out." Then **immediately, she fell down at his feet and died.** And the young men came in and found her dead, and carrying her out, buried her by her husband. So great fear came upon all the Church and upon all who heard these things.*

### *Ephesians 4:25-32*

*Therefore, **you must stop telling lies**, "Let each one of you speak truth with his neighbor," for we are members of the* *same Body. **"Be angry, and do not sin"**: do not let the sun go down on your anger, nor give an Open Door to the Devil to come in. **Let him who stole steal no longer,** but rather let him labor, working with his hands what is good, that he may have something to give him who has need. Let no corrupt word proceed out of your mouth, but what is good for necessary edification, that it may impart Grace to the hearers. **And <u>do not grieve the Holy Spirit of GOD</u>**, by whom you were sealed for the day of redemption. **Let all bitterness, wrath, anger, loud arguing, and evil speaking be put away from you, along with all wickedness. And be kind to one another, tenderhearted, forgiving one another, even as GOD in the Messiah forgave you.***

The reason Paul wrote about not participating in all of the negative behavior he described is two-fold. First, is that it opens the door to the enemy with an opportunity to cause all manner of destruction in your life. Second, and most important, is because the Holy Spirit lives inside you, so you are forcing Her to experience the wrongs you are doing along with you, and as a result, you are "Grieving" the Holy Spirit of GOD. Isaiah said it this way:

*Isaiah 63:10*
*But **they rebelled and <u>grieved the Holy Spirit, so the LORD turned against them as an enemy</u>** and fought against them.*

You may recall earlier in Chapter Two, when we recognized that the person of "*Wisdom*" is actually The Holy Spirit. We can see here in Proverbs a similar consequence for sinning against Wisdom.

*Proverbs 8:36*
**<u>Wisdom</u>** speaking: *"But **<u>he who sins against Me wrongs his own Soul; all those who hate Me, love death.</u>**"*

# CHAPTER ELEVEN

# GOD THE MOTHER

There are so many Scriptures describing the role that the Holy Spirit plays in our daily lives. Now, many of us know and can easily accept that we are often referred to as GOD's Children. Throughout history, who has been the primary Nurturer, Comforter, Teacher, and Guide for children? Well, that would most definitely be mothers! Marriage and family life are both modeled after the behavior and characteristics of GOD towards us. So, would it not make perfect sense for "God the Mother" to come and care for Their new Children, the ones She just gave Birth to when we were Born-Again?

Let me ask you this, who else could possibly care for so many Children all over the world better than a Divine Mother? Women have a Natural ability to multitask that is unmatched, making them uniquely qualified to take care of children. Have you ever noticed how mothers can be performing multiple tasks, be involved in a conversation, then hear several children speaking at the same time, and still understand them all? Well, that is just how women are hardwired in their brains. I cannot tell you how many times I have seen this happen around me, and I am still always amazed at how their minds work. Now imagine if a Mother had an infinite capacity to hear an unlimited number of Her Children. That is who the Holy Spirit is, the Divine Mother, with the ability to listen to all of us who are Her Children, at the same time, and still understand and communicate with us all.

Now, I know this may seem like a strange concept for some of you. But, I find it interesting that it is so easy for some of you to accept the terms like "Mother Nature" or "Mother Earth", "Gaia" from Greek culture, "Isis" from Egyptian culture, or "Shakti" from

Hinduism, just to name a few, but many people will still think that this particular idea seems unusual. All of these "deities" I have just mentioned are "female goddesses" that people have attributed to the Creation of the world and of Humans. Well, the general idea was right, but it is simply that they gave the credit, intentionally or otherwise, to the wrong mother deity.

Next, I will list out several Scriptures describing the attributes and roles of the Holy Spirit in our lives, and you will be able to clearly see the similarities to the many of the characteristics and parts our own mothers play in our lives. Additionally, you will see that there are several traits that could only be attributed to Her, the Holy Spirit. So, now let's get back to who the Holy Spirit is to us according to the Scriptures, and how She interacts with us on a daily basis once we are Born-Again and become Her Children.

## How does the Holy Spirit work within us?

# CHAPTER TWELVE

# THE PROMISE OF THE HOLY SPIRIT

There was an exciting event that occurred surrounding the Holy Spirit coming to stay within us. You see, Jesus asked the Father and actually had Him "Promise" to send the Holy Spirit to us, that She would reside in us, Comfort us, Teach us, and Empower us to do the Will of GOD. This was meant to be the evidence to Confirm in us of the Guarantee (down-payment) of our Salvation, and was also the evidence that all three (the Father, the Son Jesus, and the Holy Spirit) reside in us, will fellowship with us, and guide us any time we needed Them, or wanted to reach out to Them.

### *Acts 1:1-8*

Luke, the Medical Doctor, writing: *In my former book, Theophilus, I wrote about all that Jesus began to do and to teach until the day He was taken up to Heaven, after **He** (Jesus) **gave instructions through the Holy Spirit to the Apostles He had chosen.** After His suffering, He presented Himself to them alive and gave many convincing proofs. He appeared to them over a period of forty days and spoke about the Kingdom of GOD. On one occasion, while Jesus was with them, He gave them this Command: "Do not leave Jerusalem, but wait for the **Promise of the Father**; that which you have heard Me say, 'For John truly baptized with water, but **you will be baptized with the Holy Spirit.'** not many days from now." Then they gathered around Him and asked Him, "Lord, are You at this time going to restore The Kingdom to Israel?" **Jesus said to them:** "It is not for you to know the times or dates the Father has set by His own Authority. But **you will receive Power when the Holy Spirit comes on you, and you will be My witnesses in Jerusalem, and in all Judea and Samaria, and to the ends of the Earth."***

<u>*Acts 2:1-39*</u>

*When the Day of Pentecost had arrived, they were all together in one place. And suddenly there came a sound from Heaven, like a gust of a rushing wind, and it filled the whole house where they were sitting. Then there appeared to them divided **tongues, like Fire, and settled upon each one of them. And they were all filled with the Holy Spirit and began to speak with other languages, as the Holy Spirit gave them the words to speak.***

*Now there were staying in Jerusalem, GOD-fearing Jews from every Nation under Heaven. When they heard this sound, a crowd came together in bewilderment, because each one heard their own language being spoken. Utterly amazed, they asked: "Aren't all these who are speaking Galileans? Then how is it that **each of us hears them in our native language**, in which we were born? Parthians, Medes, and Elamites; those inhabiting Mesopotamia, Judea also and Cappadocia, Pontus and Asia, Phrygia and Pamphylia, Egypt and the parts of Libya near Cyrene; and those visiting from Rome – both Jews and converts to Judaism – Cretans and Arabs – **we hear them declaring the Wonders of GOD in our own native languages!"** Amazed and perplexed, they asked one another, "What does this mean?" Some, however, made fun of them and said, "They have had too much wine to drink."*

*Then Peter stood up with the Eleven, raised his voice, and addressed the crowd: "Fellow Jews and all of you who are residing in Jerusalem, let me explain this to you; listen carefully to what I say. These people are not drunk, as you suppose. It's only nine o'clock in the morning! No, **this is what was spoken by the Prophet Joel:***

*'**In the Last Days, GOD says, I will pour out My Spirit on all people. Your sons and daughters will Prophesy; your young men will see Visions; your old men will Dream Dreams. Even on My servants, both men and women,***

*I will pour out My Spirit in those days, and they will Prophesy.* *I will show Wonders in the Heavens above and Signs on the Earth below, blood and fire and billows of smoke. The sun will be turned to darkness and the moon to blood before the coming of the great and glorious Day of the LORD. And everyone who calls on the name of the LORD will be saved.'*

*"Fellow Israelites, listen to this: Jesus of Nazareth was a man Confirmed to you by GOD, by Miracles, Wonders, and Signs, which GOD did among you through Him, as you yourselves know. Him, being delivered by GOD's deliberate plan and foreknowledge; and you, with the help of wicked men, crucified and put Him to death. But GOD raised Him from the dead, freeing Him from the agony of death, because it was impossible for death to keep its hold on Him. David said about Him:*

*'I saw the LORD always before Me. Because He is at My right-hand, I will not be shaken. Therefore, My heart is glad and My tongue rejoices; My body also will rest in Hope, because You will not abandon Me to the realm of the dead, You will not let your Holy One see decay. You have made known to Me the paths of life; You will fill Me with Joy in Your presence.'*

*"Fellow Israelites, I can tell you confidently that the patriarch David died and was buried, and his tomb is here to this day. But he was a Prophet and knew that GOD had promised him on oath that He would place one of David's descendants on his throne. Seeing what was to come, he spoke of the resurrection of the Messiah, that He was not abandoned to the realm of the dead, nor did His body see decay. GOD has raised this Jesus to life, and we are all witnesses of it. Exalted to the right-hand of GOD, **He has received from the Father the Promise of the Holy Spirit and has poured out what you now see and hear.** For David did not ascend to Heaven, and yet he said, 'The*

LORD *said to my Lord: "Sit at My right-hand until I make Your enemies a footstool for Your feet."' Therefore, let all Israel be assured of this:* **GOD has made this Jesus, whom you crucified, both Lord and Messiah."** *When the people heard this, they were cut to the heart and said to Peter and the other Apostles, "Brothers, what shall we do?"* **Peter replied, "Repent and be baptized, every one of you, in the name of Jesus, the Messiah, for the forgiveness of your sins. And <u>you will receive the Gift of the Holy Spirit</u>. The <u>Promise</u> is for you and your children and for all who are far off – for all whom the LORD our GOD will call."**

## Acts 15:1-11

*Certain people came down from Judea to Antioch and were teaching the Believers: "Unless you are circumcised, according to the custom taught by Moses, you cannot be saved." This brought Paul and Barnabas into sharp dispute and debate with them. So, Paul and Barnabas were appointed, along with some other Believers, to go up to Jerusalem to see the Apostles and Elders about this question. The Church sent them on their way, and as they traveled through Phoenicia and Samaria, they told how the Gentiles had been converted. This news made all the Believers very glad. When they came to Jerusalem, they were welcomed by the Church and the Apostles and Elders, to whom they reported everything GOD had done through them. Then some of the Believers who belonged to the party of the Pharisees stood up and said, "The Gentiles must be circumcised and be required to keep the Law of Moses." The Apostles and Elders met to consider this question. After much discussion,* **Peter got up and addressed them: "Brothers, you know that some time ago GOD made a choice among you that the Gentiles might hear from my lips the message of the Gospel and believe.**

*GOD, who knows the heart, showed that He accepted them by giving the Holy Spirit to them, just as He did to us. He did not discriminate between them and us, for He purified their hearts by Faith. Now then, why do you try to Test GOD by putting a yoke on the necks of Gentiles that our ancestors nor we have been able to bear? No! We believe it is through the Grace of our Lord Jesus that we are saved, just as they are."*

### Romans 9:1
*I speak the truth in Christ; I am not lying, my conscience Confirms it* (bears witness) *through the Holy Spirit –*

### 2 Corinthians 1:19-22
*For the Son of GOD, Christ Jesus, the One who was preached among you by us – by me and Silas and Timothy – was not "Yes" and "No," but in Him, it has always been "Yes." For no matter how many promises GOD has made, they are "Yes" in Christ. And so, through Him, the "Amen" is spoken by us to the Glory of GOD. Now it is GOD who makes both us and you stand firm in the Messiah; the One who anointed us, <u>set a seal of ownership on us, and given the Promise of The Spirit in our hearts as a down-payment, guaranteeing what is to come.</u>*

### 2 Corinthians 3:1-18
*Are we beginning to approve ourselves again? Or do we need, like some people, letters of recommendation to you or from you? You yourselves are our letter, written on our hearts, known and read by everyone. You show that you*

*are a letter of Christ, the result of our ministry, written not with ink but with The Spirit of the living GOD, not on tablets of stone but on tablets of Human hearts.* Such confidence we have through the Messiah before GOD. Not that we are competent in ourselves to claim anything for ourselves, but our competence comes from GOD. *And GOD has made us competent as ministers of a New Covenant – not of the letter but of The Spirit; for the letter kills, but The Spirit gives Life.*

Now if the ministry that brought death, having been engraved in letters on stone, came with glory, so that the Israelites could not look steadily at the face of Moses because of its glory, though it was fading away, **will not the ministry of The Spirit be even more glorious?** If the ministry that brought condemnation was glorious, **how much more glorious is the ministry that brings righteousness!** For what was glorious has no glory now in comparison with the surpassing glory. And if what was fading away came with glory, how much greater is the Glory of that which lasts! Therefore, **since we have such a Hope, we are very bold.** We are not like Moses, who would put a veil over his face to prevent the Israelites from seeing the end of what was fading away. But their minds were made dull, for to this day the same veil remains when the Old Covenant is read. It has not been removed, because only in the Messiah is it taken away. Even to this day, when Moses is read, a veil covers their hearts. But whenever anyone turns to the Lord, the veil is taken away. **Now the LORD is The Spirit, and where the Spirit of the LORD is, there is freedom. But we all, with an unveiled face, observing as in a mirror the Glory of the LORD, are being transformed into the same image from glory to glory, just as by the Spirit of the LORD.**

## 2 Corinthians 5:1-5

*For we know that if our earthly residence* (physical body), *this tent, is destroyed, we have a building from GOD, a residence not made with hands, eternal in the Heavens. For in this we sigh in grief, earnestly desiring to be clothed with our residence, which is from Heaven, if indeed, having been clothed, we shall not be found naked. For we who are in this tent sigh in grief, being burdened, not because we want to be unclothed, but further clothed, that mortality may be swallowed up by Life.* **Now the One who has prepared us for this very thing is GOD, who also has given us The Spirit as a down payment.** *Therefore, we are always confident, knowing that while we are at home in this body, we are absent from the Lord. For we Walk by Faith, not by sight. Now we are confident, and well pleased, but would rather be absent from the body and to be present with the Lord.*

## Galatians 3:1-14

*O foolish Galatians! Who has bewitched you that you should not obey the truth, before whose own eyes Jesus, the Messiah, was clearly portrayed among you as crucified? This only I want to learn from you:* **Did you receive The Spirit by the works of the Law, or by the hearing of Faith? Are you so foolish? Having begun in the Spirit, are you now being made perfect by the Flesh?** *Have you suffered so many things in vain – if indeed it was in vain?* **Therefore, the One who supplies The Spirit to you and works miracles among you, is it done by the works of the Law, or by the hearing of Faith?** *So also, "Abraham believed GOD, and it was accounted to him for righteousness." Therefore, know that only those who are of Faith, these are sons and daughters of Abraham. And the Scripture, foreseeing that GOD would justify the*

*Gentiles by Faith, preached the Gospel to Abraham beforehand, saying, "In you, all the Nations shall be blessed." So then those who are of the Faith are blessed with believing Abraham.*

*For as many as are of the works of the Law are under the Curse; for it is written, "Cursed is everyone who does not continue in all things which are written in the Book of the Law, to do them." But that no one is justified by the Law in the sight of GOD is evident, for "the just shall live by Faith." Yet the Law is not of Faith, but "the man who does them shall live by them."* **The Messiah has redeemed us from the Curse of the Law,** *having become a Curse for us, for it is written: "Cursed is everyone who hangs on a tree",* **that the blessing of Abraham might come** *upon the Gentiles in Christ Jesus,* **that we might receive the Promise of The Spirit through Faith.**

*Ephesians 1:1-23*

*Paul, an Apostle of Jesus, the Messiah, by the Will of GOD, to the Believers who are in Ephesus, and faithful in Christ Jesus: Grace to you and Peace from God our Father and the Lord Jesus, the Messiah.*

*Blessed be the God and Father of our Lord Jesus, the Messiah, who has blessed us with every spiritual blessing in the heavenly places in Christ, just as He chose us in Him before the foundation of the world, that we should be holy and without blame before Him in Love, having predestined us to adoption as both sons and daughters, and heirs through Jesus, the Messiah, to Himself, according to the delight of His Will, to the praise of the Glory of His Grace, by which He bestowed upon us in the One whom He loves, in whom we have redemption through His Blood, the forgiveness of sins, according to the riches of His Grace which He lavished upon us in all Wisdom and Understanding, having made known to us the Mystery of His Will, according to His delight which He purposed in Himself, that in the administration of the completion of the times He might gather together in One all things in Christ, that which is in Heaven and which are on Earth, in Him whom also we have obtained an inheritance, being predestined according to the purpose of Him who works all things according to the counsel of His Will, that we who first trusted in the Messiah should be to the praise of His Glory. In Him you also trusted, after you heard the Word of Truth, the Gospel of your salvation; in whom also,* **having believed, you were sealed with the Holy Spirit of Promise, who is the assurance of our inheritance** *until the redemption of the purchased possession, to the praise of His Glory.*

*Therefore I also, after I heard of your Faith in the Lord Jesus and your love for all the Believers, do not cease to give thanks for you, making mention of you in my prayers:* ***that the God of our Lord Jesus, the Messiah, the Father of Glory, may give to you the Spirit of Wisdom and Revelation in the Knowledge of Him*** (the Father)***, the eyes of your hearts being enlightened; that you may know what the Hope of His Calling is, what are the riches of the Glory of His inheritance in the Believers, and what is the exceeding greatness of His Power toward us who believe***, *according to the working of His mighty Power which He worked in Christ when He* (the Father) *raised Him* (Jesus) *from the dead and seated Him at His right-hand* (next to the Father's Throne) *in the heavenly places, far above all principality and authority and power and dominion, and every name that is named, not only in this age but also in that which is to come. And He* (Father) *put all things under His* (Jesus') *feet, and gave Him to be head over all things to the Church, which is His Body, the fullness of Him who fills all in all.*

## 2 Thessalonians 2:13-17

*But we have an obligation to give thanks to GOD always for you, beloved brothers and sisters, by the Lord,* **because from the beginning GOD chose you for salvation, through the sanctification by The Spirit,** *and Faith in the Truth, to which He also called you through our Gospel, for the obtaining of the Glory of our Lord Jesus, the Messiah. So then, brothers and sisters, stand firm and hold to the Traditions which you were taught, whether by word of mouth or by our letters.* **Now may our Lord Jesus, the Messiah Himself, and God our Father, who having loved us and given us eternal comfort and good Hope through Grace, comfort your hearts and strengthen you in every good word and deed.**

## Hebrews 10:11-18

*And indeed, every priest stands ministering daily and repeatedly offering the same sacrifices, which can never take away sins. But this One* (Jesus)*, after He had offered one sacrifice for sins forever, sat down at the right-hand of God* (the Father)*, from that time waiting till His enemies are made His* (Jesus')* footstool.* **For by one offering, He has perfected forever those who are being sanctified. But the Holy Spirit also Confirms with us; saying before, "This is the covenant that I will make with them after those days, says the LORD: I will put My laws into their hearts, and in their minds, I will write them." and also, "Their sins and their lawless deeds I will remember no more."** *Now where there is forgiveness of these, there is no longer a need for an offering for sin.*

# CHAPTER THIRTEEN

# THE HOLY SPIRIT: GLORIFIES JESUS

I find it very interesting that the Holy Spirit's actions towards Her Son are very similar to how "Good Moms" will act towards their own children. They will lift up their own child and draw attention to them rather than to themselves. They look at it like they do not have to draw attention to themselves, because if their child does well, it reflects positively on the way they raised them, thus also reflecting a positive view of themselves. More importantly, they are happy to give glory to their child because of the love and pride they feel for them. I believe this is a very similar situation, and the Holy Spirit has shown that She feels that same pride and joy for Her Son, and all He has accomplished, not only for us, but also for the Kingdom of GOD.

Now, the flip side of this is something that we all need to understand; there will be consequences from the Holy Spirit for those who attack Her Son, or mock the sacrifices He made and all He had to endure for us. Just in this same way, any Good Mom would defend their own child if they were being attacked.

### John 15:26

Jesus speaking: *"**When the Comforter comes,** whom I shall send to you from the Father, **the Spirit of Truth** who proceeds from the Father, **She will testify of Me.**

### John 16:12-15

Jesus speaking: *"I have so much more to tell you, but it is too much for you to accept now. But **when the Spirit of Truth comes, She will lead you into all Truth. She will not speak of Herself,** but whatever She hears, that She will *speak, and will tell you what will happen in the future.* **She will glorify Me by telling you what She receives from Me.** *All that the Father possesses is Mine, that is why I said that the She will tell you what She receives from Me."*


## Romans 1:1-6

*Paul, a servant of Jesus, the Messiah, called to be an Apostle, having been set apart for the Gospel of GOD, which was promised before through His Prophets in the Holy Scriptures, concerning His Son, who was born of the seed of David according to the Flesh, and* **declared to be the Son of GOD with Power by way of the Spirit of Holiness,** *by the resurrection from the dead: Jesus Christ our Lord; through whom we have received Grace and Apostleship for obedience to the Faith among all Nations for His name, among whom you also are the called of Jesus, the Messiah;*


## Hebrews 6:1-6

*Therefore, leaving the discussion of the basic principles of the Messiah, let us go on to the place of maturity, not laying again the foundation of repentance from dead works and faith toward GOD, of the doctrine of ceremonial washing, of laying on of hands, of the resurrection of the dead, and of eternal judgment. And this we will do if GOD permits.* **For it is impossible for those who were once enlightened, and have tasted the Heavenly Gift, and have become partakers of the Holy Spirit, and have tasted the good Word of GOD and the Powers of the age to come – and then having fallen away – to renew them again to repentance, since they crucify again for themselves the Son of GOD, and put Him to an open shame.**

## Hebrews 10:26-31

*For if we intentionally sin after we have received the Knowledge of the Truth, there no longer remains a sacrifice for sins, but a certain fearful expectation of Judgment, and fiery indignation which will devour the adversaries. Anyone who has rejected Moses' Law dies without mercy on the testimony of two or three witnesses.* **Of how much worse punishment, do you suppose, will they be thought worthy who has trampled the Son of GOD underfoot, counted the Blood of the covenant by which they were sanctified a commonplace thing, and insulted the Spirit of Grace? For we know the One who said, "Vengeance is Mine, I will repay," and again, "The LORD will judge His people." It is a fearful thing to fall into the hands of the Living GOD.**

## 1 John 5:1-12

*All who believe that Jesus is the Messiah is born of GOD, and everyone who loves the Father who bore Him, also loves the Child who is born of Him. By this, we know that we love the Children of GOD, when we love GOD and keep His Commandments. For this is the Love of GOD, that we keep His Commandments. And His Commandments are not burdensome. For everyone who is born of GOD overcomes the world. And this is the victory that has overcome the world – our Faith.* **Now, who are those who overcome the world, if not them who believe that Jesus is the Son of GOD?**

**This is the One who came by water and blood – Jesus, the Messiah; not only by water, but by water and blood. And The Spirit is the One who testifies, because The Spirit is Truth. For there are three that testify: The Spirit, the water, and the blood – and these three are One.**

*If we receive the testimony of men, the testimony of GOD is greater; for this is the testimony of GOD, that He has testified concerning His Son. He who believes in the Son of GOD has the testimony in himself; he who does not believe GOD has made Him a liar, because he has not believed the testimony that GOD has given of His Son. And this is the testimony, that GOD has given us Eternal Life, and this life is in His Son. He who has the Son has this life; he who does not have the Son of GOD does not have this life.*

# CHAPTER FOURTEEN

# THE HOLY SPIRIT: EMPOWERS US

Jesus told His Apostles and Disciples, before He ascended back into Heaven, that although they were Born-Again, He was going to send the Holy Spirit and that She would provide them with Power to Walk out this life and live as a victorious Believer. This Power not only flows into us, but also flows out of us to others, and is also used to fight against the Evil Ones. There are many symbols given to us in the Bible to illustrate this Power: Anointing Oil, Living Water, and Purifying Fire. This Power is given to us as Believers so we can strengthen, encourage, and help each other, not only for us to show the Power of GOD so we can draw others to Jesus, the Messiah, but also for us to have victory over the world, and the Evil Ones in it.

The Holy Spirit manifests this Power in several ways:

**First**, with this Power She regenerates us from the _old person_ we were, and helps us become the _new person_ we need to become—more like Her Son Jesus. The word _Sanctification_ essentially means _"The process of becoming holy."_ You see, this is a journey, and every day that goes by that we continue to do our part, the Holy Spirit will work within us and help us improve and become "better". Some people assume, incorrectly, that once we are Born-Again, we will not sin any longer. This is just not the case, and it is not even Biblical. Even Paul the Apostle, who wrote the majority of the New Testament, shared his struggle with us in Romans 7:19 when he said, _"For the good that I want to do, I do not do; but the evil I do not want to do, that I practice."_ So, if Paul, who was anointed and powerful in the Spirit, still struggled with sin, how is it that you think you should be perfect? Remember, _"We all sin and fall short of the Glory of GOD"_.

We just need to do our part Daily – Read, Pray, Seek, Ask, Fight, Repeat – and the Holy Spirit will do Her part. And if you stumble, get up, dust yourself off, ask for forgiveness, and keep Walking.

**Second**, She empowers us for Ministry by enabling us to Teach and Speak to others about Jesus, through Wisdom, Knowledge, and Understanding – because <u>She *is*</u> the Spirit of Wisdom, the Spirit of Knowledge, and the Spirit of Understanding. She also provides us with the Boldness and Courage to speak the Word of GOD and the Will of GOD when prompted. We are directed to speak to others with love, and not condemnation or judgment. As the Scripture says, "*If I have a Faith that can move mountains, but do not have Love, I am nothing.*" Jesus gave us the example of always speaking to "Sinners" with love and compassion, but He only spoke down to the "Self-righteous" and "Cold-hearted" with judgment. We also are to allow the Holy Spirit to be the One discerning for us regarding who we are supposed to speak with, as the Scripture says in Matthew 7:6, "*Do not give that which is holy to the dogs, nor throw your pearls before pigs, lest they will trample them under their feet, then turn, and tear you in pieces.*" Anyone who has ever tried to share the Holy Scriptures or their Pearls of Wisdom with an Unbeliever who is not ready to hear, truly understands what this Verse is saying, because they will stomp on the message, and attack you. Always "Ask" the Holy Spirit who you should speak with, and wait for an answer! Silence does not mean "Yes". Only do the things that GOD has "Called" you to do and "Gifted" you to do… or you will fail.

**Third**, our Gifts are manifested by this Power we are given, which allows us to show the unbelieving world that GOD is alive and dwells within us, and that the Word of GOD is true – because She is the Spirit of Truth and will Teach us all about Her Son Jesus, and remind us of His Words. This topic regarding the "Gifts of the Holy Spirit" will be discussed in more detail in the Chapter with that title.

**Fourth**, we are given the Power to exercise the Authority we have been granted. In the name of Jesus, and with the Power of the Holy Spirit, we can cast out the Evil Ones (*Demons*) from others and from our own lives, break curses, repel witchcraft, and not only fight off their attacks, but advance and take back territory they once held. I will review this topic in much more detail later in the Chapter on "Spiritual Warfare".

The following are several Scriptures dealing with how the Holy Spirit Empowers us and Enables us to do all that we need to do for the Kingdom of GOD. I would like to suggest you would take the time and read through them all completely, and not just the highlighted parts. You will get a lot more out of it if you do.

*John 7:37-39*
*On the last and greatest day of the Festival, Jesus stood and said in a loud voice, "Let anyone who thirsts come to Me and drink. Whoever believes in Me, as Scripture has said: 'Out of their hearts will flow rivers of Living Water.'" Jesus was talking about the Holy Spirit. The Spirit had not yet been given to the people, because Jesus had not yet been raised to glory. But later, those who believed in Jesus would receive the Holy Spirit.*

*Luke 4:18*

Jesus speaking: ***"The Spirit of the L<small>ORD</small> is upon Me***, *who has anointed Me to proclaim good news to the poor; has sent me to Heal the brokenhearted, to proclaim liberty to those captive and recovery of sight for the blind, to set the Oppressed free."*

*Acts 8:26-40*

*Now an Angel of the L<small>ORD</small> said to Philip, "Go towards the south, to the road that goes down from Jerusalem to Gaza; the desert road." So, he started out, and on his way, he met an Ethiopian eunuch, a prominent official in charge of all the treasury of Candace, the Queen of the Ethiopians. This man had gone to Jerusalem to worship, and on his way home was sitting in his chariot, reading the Book of Isaiah the Prophet. **The Holy Spirit told Philip, "Go to that chariot and stay near it."** Then Philip ran up to the chariot and heard the man reading Isaiah the Prophet. "Do you understand what you are reading?" Philip asked. "How can I," he said, "unless someone explains it to me?" So, he invited Philip to come up and sit with him. This is the passage of Scripture the eunuch was reading:*

*"He was led like a sheep to the slaughter, and as a Lamb before its shearer is silent, so He did not open His mouth. In His humiliation, He was deprived of justice. Who can speak of His descendants? For His life was taken from the Earth."*

*The eunuch asked Philip, "Tell me, please, who is the Prophet talking about, himself or someone else?" Then Philip began with that very passage of Scripture and told him the Good News about Jesus. As they traveled along the road, they came to some water, and the eunuch said, "Look, here is water. What stands in the way of my being* baptized?" Then Philip said, "If you believe with all your heart, you may." And he answered and said, "I believe that Jesus, the Messiah, is the Son of GOD." And he gave orders to stop the chariot. Then both Philip and the eunuch went down into the water, and Philip baptized him. When they came up out of the water, **the Spirit of the LORD suddenly took Philip away**, and the eunuch did not see him again, but went on his way rejoicing. **Philip, however, appeared at Ashdod** (about 30 miles away) **and traveled about, preaching the Gospel in all the towns until he reached Caesarea.**

### Matthew 3:11

John the Baptist speaking: *"I indeed baptize you in water unto repentance, but He who is coming after me is mightier than I, whose sandals I am not worthy to carry.* **He** (Jesus) **will baptize you in the Holy Spirit and Fire."**

### Matthew 12:28

Jesus speaking: *"But **if I cast out Demons by the Spirit of GOD, surely the Kingdom of GOD has come upon you.**"*

### Matthew 28:18-20

*And Jesus came and spoke to them, saying, "All Authority has been given to Me in Heaven and on Earth. Go therefore and* **make Disciples of all the Nations, baptizing them in the name of the Father and of the Son and of the Holy Spirit,** *teaching them to observe all things that I have commanded you; and lo, I am with you all your days, to the completion of this age."*

## Mark 1:7-8

*And John the Baptist preached, saying, "There comes One after me who is mightier than I, whose sandal straps I am not worthy to stoop down and untie. I indeed baptize you in water, but **He will baptize you in the Holy Spirit.**"*

## Luke 1:13-15

*But the Angel said to him, "Do not be afraid, Zacharias, for your prayer has been heard, and your wife Elizabeth will bear you a son, and you shall call his name John* (the Baptist). *And you will have Joy and gladness, and many will rejoice at his Birth. For he will be great in the sight of the LORD, and shall drink neither wine nor strong drink. **He will be filled with the Holy Spirit, even from his mother's womb.**"*

## Luke 4:14-19,22

*Then Jesus returned **in the Power of The Spirit** to Galilee, and news of Him went out through all the surrounding region. And He taught in their Synagogues, being glorified by all. So, He came to Nazareth, where He had been brought up. And as His custom was, He went into the Synagogue on the Sabbath day and stood up to read* (in Hebrew). *And He was handed the Book of the Prophet Isaiah. And when He had opened the book, He found the place where it was written:*

*"**The Spirit of the LORD is upon Me, because the LORD has anointed Me to preach the Good News of the Gospel to the poor.** He has sent Me to Heal the brokenhearted, **to proclaim a Pardon to the captives** and recovery of sight to the blind, **to set free those who are Oppressed;** to proclaim the acceptable year of the LORD."*

*So, **all bore witness** (Confirmed by the Spirit) **to Him, and marveled at the gracious words which proceeded out of His mouth.***

### John 7:37-39
*On the Last Day, that great day of the feast, Jesus stood and cried out, saying, "If anyone thirsts, let them come to Me and drink. **Those who believe in Me**, as the Scripture has said, **out of their heart** will flow rivers of **Living Water**." But this He spoke **concerning The Spirit**, whom those who believe in Him would receive; for The Spirit was not yet given, because Jesus was not yet glorified.*

### Acts 4:3,5,7-13
*They seized Peter and John, but because it was evening, they put them in jail until the next day. Then it came to pass on the next day, they gathered together their rulers, elders, and scribes in Jerusalem. They had Peter and John brought before them and began to question them: "By what power or what name did you do this?" Then **Peter, filled with the Holy Spirit, said to them:** "Rulers and Elders of the people! If we are being called to account today for an act of kindness shown to a man who was lame and are being asked how he was Healed, then know this, you and all the people of Israel: **It is by the name of the Messiah, Jesus of Nazareth, but whom you crucified, but whom GOD raised from the dead, that this man stands before you Healed.** Jesus is 'the stone you builders rejected, which has become the cornerstone.' **Salvation is found in no one else,** for there is no other name under Heaven given to mankind by which we must be saved." When they saw the **courage of Peter and John** and realized that they were unschooled, ordinary men, they were astonished and they took note that **these men had been with Jesus**.*

*And being let go, they went to their own companions and reported all that the chief priests and elders had said to them. So when they heard that, they raised their voice to GOD as one unified voice and said: "**Sovereign LORD, You who made Heaven and Earth and the Sea, and all that is in them, <u>spoke by the Holy Spirit through the mouth of your servant, our ancestor David</u>:***

*'Why did the Nations rage, and the people plot vain things? The kings of the Earth took their stand, and the rulers were gathered together against the LORD and against His Anointed Messiah.'*

*For truly against Your Holy Servant Jesus, whom You anointed, both Herod and Pontius Pilate, with the Gentiles and the people of Israel, were gathered together to do whatever Your hand and Your purpose determined before to be done. Now, LORD, look on their threats, and **grant to Your servants that with all boldness they may speak Your Word, by stretching out Your hand to Heal, and that Signs and Wonders may be done through the name of Your Holy Servant Jesus." And when they had prayed, the place where they were assembled together was shaken; and <u>they were all filled with the Holy Spirit, and they spoke the Word of GOD with boldness</u>.***

*Acts 6:1-10*

*Now in those days, when the number of the Believers were multiplying, there arose complaints by the Greek-speaking Jews against the Hebrew-speaking Jews, because their widows were being neglected in the daily distribution of food. Then the Twelve* (Apostles) *summoned the multitude of the Disciples and said, "It is not desirable that we should leave the Word of GOD and serve tables. Therefore,* *brothers and sisters, seek out from among you seven men of good reputation, **full of the Holy Spirit and Wisdom**, whom we may appoint over this business; but we will give ourselves continually to prayer and to the ministry of the Word." And the saying pleased the whole multitude. And they chose **Stephen, a man full of Faith and the Holy Spirit**, and Philip, Prochorus, Nicanor, Timon, Parmenas, and Nicolas, a convert to Judaism from Antioch, whom they set before the Apostles; and when they had prayed, they Laid Hands on them. Then the Word of GOD spread, and the number of the Disciples multiplied greatly in Jerusalem, and a great many of the priests were obedient to the Faith. And Stephen, **full of Grace and Power, performed many great Wonders and Signs among the people.** Then there arose some from what is called the Synagogue of the Roman Freedmen, including Cyrenians, Alexandrians, and those from Cilicia and Asia, disputing with Stephen. But **they were unable to oppose him and argue against the <u>Wisdom that the Holy Spirit gave him as he spoke</u>.***

### Acts 8:5-25

*Now Philip, having gone down to a City of Samaria, was preaching to them about Jesus, the Messiah. **The crowds all paid close attention to what Philip said when they heard his words and saw the miraculous Signs he performed. For <u>unclean spirits</u>, crying with a loud voice, <u>came out of many of those who were Possessed</u>; and many who were <u>paralyzed and lame were Healed</u>. And then there was great Joy in that City.***

*But there was a certain man called Simon, who previously practiced sorcery in the City and astonished the people of Samaria, claiming that he was someone great, to whom they all listened to, from the least to the greatest, saying,*

*"This man is the great power of god." And they listened to him because he had amazed them with his sorceries for a long time. But when they believed Philip as he preached the things concerning the Kingdom of GOD and the name of Jesus, the Messiah, both men and women were baptized. Then Simon himself also believed; and when he was baptized, he continued steadfast with Philip and was himself amazed, seeing the miracles and Signs done through Philip.*

*Now when the Apostles who were at Jerusalem heard that Samaria had received the Word of GOD, they sent **Peter and John** to them, who, when they had come down, **prayed for them that they might receive the Holy Spirit. For She had not yet fallen upon any of them.** They had only been baptized in the name of the Lord Jesus. **Then <u>the Apostles Laid Hands on them, and they received the Holy Spirit</u>.** And when Simon saw that **through the laying on of the Apostles' hands the Holy Spirit was given,** he offered them money, saying, **"Give me this Power also, that anyone on whom I lay hands may receive the Holy Spirit."** But **Peter** said to him, "May you and your money be destroyed, because you thought that the Gift of GOD could be purchased with money! You have neither part nor portion in this matter, for your heart is not right in the sight of GOD. Repent therefore of this your wickedness, and pray GOD if perhaps the thought of your heart may be forgiven you. **<u>For I see</u>** (in the Spirit) that you are poisoned by bitterness and bound by iniquity." Then Simon answered and said, "Pray to the LORD for me, that none of the things which you have spoken may come upon me." So, when they had testified and preached the Word of the LORD, they returned to Jerusalem, preaching the Gospel in many villages of the Samaritans.*

*Acts 9:17-18*

*And Ananias went his way and entered the house; and **laying his hands on him,** he said, "Brother Saul, **the Lord Jesus**, who appeared to you on the road as you came, **has sent me that you may receive your sight and be filled with the Holy Spirit.**" Immediately there fell from his eyes something like scales, and he received his sight at once, and he arose and was baptized.*

*Acts 10:44-46*

*While Peter was still speaking these words, **the Holy Spirit fell upon all who heard the message**. The Jewish Believers who had come with Peter were astonished that the Gift of the Holy Spirit had been poured out even on Gentiles. For they heard them speaking in Tongues and praising GOD.*

*Acts 10:38*

*GOD anointed Jesus of Nazareth with the Holy Spirit and with Power, who went about doing good and Healing all who were Oppressed by the Devil, for GOD was with Him.*

*Acts 11:22-24*

*Then news of these things came to the ears of the Church in Jerusalem, and they sent out Barnabas to go as far as Antioch. When he came and had seen the Grace of GOD, he was glad and encouraged them all that with purpose of heart, they should continue with the Lord. For he was a good man, full of the Holy Spirit and of Faith. And a great many people were added to the Lord.*

## Acts 13:1-12

Now **in the Church** at Antioch, **there were Prophets and Teachers:** Barnabas, Simeon called Niger, Lucius of Cyrene, Manaen – who had been brought up with Herod the Tetrarch – and Saul. While they were worshiping the LORD and fasting, **the Holy Spirit said,** "Set apart for me **Barnabas and Saul for the work to which I have called them.**" So, after they had fasted and prayed, **they placed their hands on them and sent them off.**

**The two of them, sent on their way by the Holy Spirit,** went down to Seleucia and sailed from there to Cyprus. When they arrived at Salamis, **they proclaimed the Word of GOD** in the Jewish Synagogues. John was with them as their helper. They traveled through the whole island until they came to Paphos. There they met a Jewish sorcerer and false prophet named Bar-Jesus, who was an attendant of the Proconsul, Sergius Paulus. The Proconsul, an intelligent man, sent for Barnabas and Saul because he wanted to hear the Word of GOD. But Elymas, the sorcerer – for that is what his name means – opposed them and tried to turn the Proconsul from the Faith. Then Saul, who was also called **Paul, filled with the Holy Spirit,** looked straight at Elymas and **said, "You are a child of the Devil and an enemy of everything that is right!** You are full of all kinds of deceit and trickery. Will you never stop perverting the right ways of the LORD? Now the hand of the LORD is against you. **You are going to be blind for a time, not even able to see the light of the sun."** **Immediately mist and darkness came over him, and he groped about, seeking someone to lead him by the hand.** **When the Proconsul saw what had happened, he believed,** for he was amazed at the teaching about the Lord.

*Acts 13:48-52*

*Now when the Gentiles heard this, they were glad and glorified the Word of the LORD. And as many as had been appointed to Eternal Life believed.* **And the Word of the LORD was being spread throughout all the region.** *But the Jews stirred up the devout and prominent women and the chief men of the City,* **raised up persecution against Paul and Barnabas,** *and expelled them from their region. But they shook off the dust from their feet against them and came to Iconium.* **And** <u>**the Disciples were filled with Joy and with the Holy Spirit**</u>.


*Romans 15:13-19*

**May the God of Hope fill you with all Joy and Peace as you trust in Him, so that you may overflow with Hope by the Power of the Holy Spirit.**

*I myself am convinced, my brothers and sisters, that you yourselves are full of goodness, filled with Knowledge and competent to instruct one another. Yet I have written you quite boldly on some points to remind you of them again, because of the Grace that GOD gave me to be a minister of Christ Jesus to the Gentiles. He gave me the priestly duty of* **proclaiming the Gospel of GOD, so that the Gentiles might become** *an offering acceptable to GOD,* <u>**sanctified by the Holy Spirit**</u>*. Therefore, I glory in Christ Jesus in my service to GOD. I will not venture to speak of anything except what the Messiah has accomplished through me in leading the Gentiles to obey GOD by what I have said and done –* <u>**by the Power of Signs and Wonders, through the Power of the Spirit of GOD**</u>*. So, from Jerusalem all the way around to Illyricum, I have fully proclaimed the Gospel of the Messiah.*

## 1 Corinthians 2:1-16

*And I, brothers and sisters, when I came to you, did not come with excellence of speech or wisdom, proclaiming to you the testimony of GOD. For I determined not to know anything among you, except Jesus, the Messiah, and Him crucified. I was with you in weakness, in fear, and in much trembling.* **And my message and my preaching were not with persuasive words of Human wisdom, <u>but by proofs demonstrated of The Spirit and of Power</u>, that your Faith should not be based on the wisdom of men, but on the Power of GOD.**

*However, we speak Wisdom among those who are mature, yet not the wisdom of this age, nor of the rulers of this age, who are coming to nothing. But* **we speak the Wisdom of GOD in a Mystery,** *the hidden Wisdom which GOD predetermined before the ages for our glory, which none of the rulers of this age understood; for had they known, they would not have crucified the Lord of Glory. But as it is written:*

*"Eye has not seen, nor ear heard, nor have entered into the heart of man the things which GOD has prepared for those who love Him."*

**But GOD has revealed these things to us through The Spirit, for <u>The Spirit searches all things, even the deep things of GOD</u>.** *For what man knows the things of a man, except for the spirit of the man that is within him? Even so,* **no one knows the things of GOD except the Spirit of GOD. Now we have not received the spirit of the world, but The Spirit who is from GOD, <u>that we might know the things that have been freely given to us by GOD</u>. These things we also speak, not in words which man's wisdom teaches, but those <u>The Spirit teaches, comparing spiritual things with spiritual</u>. But the Natural man does not receive the things of the Spirit of GOD, for they are foolishness to him; nor can he know them, because they are spiritually discerned.**

*But he who is spiritual judges all things, yet he himself is rightly judged by no one. For, "Who has known the mind of the LORD? Who may instruct Him?"* **But we have the mind of the Messiah.**


<u>2 Corinthians 6:1-10</u>

*Now, as we work together with GOD, we urge you not to receive GOD's Grace in vain. For GOD says, "In the time of My favor, I heard you, and in the day of salvation I helped you."*

*Behold, now is the time of GOD's favor; behold, now is the day of salvation. We put no obstacles in anyone's path, so that our ministry would not be blamed. Rather, as servants of GOD, we ourselves demonstrate in every way: in great endurance; in persecutions, hardships and distresses; in beatings, in imprisonments, in riots, in hard work, in sleepless nights, in hunger;* **in purity, in Wisdom, in patience, in kindness, in the Holy Spirit, in sincere Love; in words of Truth, in the Power of GOD; with the weapons of righteousness in the right-hand and in the left;** *through glory and dishonor, through bad report and good report; truthful, yet regarded as misleading; known, yet regarded as unknown; as about to die, and yet behold, we live on; as beaten, and yet not killed; as sorrowful, yet always rejoicing; as poor, yet making many rich; as having nothing, and yet possessing all things.*


<u>Ephesians 3:1-21</u>

*For this reason, I Paul, the prisoner of Christ Jesus on behalf of you Gentiles – if indeed you have heard of the administration of the Grace of GOD that was given to me for you, how* **by Revelation the Mystery was made known to me** *– as I have briefly written already, by which, when* *you read, you may understand my knowledge in the Mystery of the Messiah – which in other generations was not made known to the sons of men, as it **has now been revealed to His holy Apostles and Prophets in the Spirit**. This Mystery is that the Gentiles are fellow heirs, members of the same Body, and also partakers of the Promise in Christ Jesus through the Gospel, of which I became a minister according to the **Gift of the Grace of GOD given to me by the effective working of GOD's Power**. To me, though I am the very least of all the Believers, **this Grace was given, to preach to the Gentiles the unsearchable riches of the Messiah, and** to bring to light for all to see what is the administration of the Mystery hidden for ages in GOD, who created all things, so that through the Church **the multifaceted Wisdom of GOD might now be made known** to the Rulers and Authorities in the heavenly places, according to the eternal purpose, which was accomplished in Christ Jesus our Lord, in whom we have boldness and access with confidence through our Faith in Him. Therefore, I ask you not to lose heart over what I am suffering for you, which is your glory.*

***For this reason, I kneel before the Father, from whom every family in the Heavens and on Earth is named, that according to the riches of His Glory, <u>He may grant you to be strengthened with Power through His Spirit in your inner being, so that the Messiah may dwell in your hearts through Faith</u>, being rooted and grounded in Love, so that you may fully have the strength to comprehend with all the Believers, what is the breadth and length and height and depth, and to know the Love of the Messiah that surpasses knowledge, so that you may be filled with all the fullness of GOD.*** *Now to One who is able to do far more abundantly than all that we ask or think, **<u>according to the Power</u>** (from the Holy Spirit) **<u>working within us</u>, to Him** (the Father) **be glory in the Church and in Christ Jesus throughout all generations, forever and ever.** Amen.*

*Ephesians 6:10-20*

*Finally, be strong in the Lord* (Jesus) *and in the Power of His might.* **Put on the complete Armor of GOD, that you may be able to stand against the strategies of the Devil. For we do not wrestle against flesh and blood, but against Principalities, against Powers, against the Rulers of the Darkness of this world, against the Evil Spirits of Wickedness in the realms of the Heavens.** *Therefore, take up the complete Armor of GOD, that you may be able to oppose them in the evil day, and having done all things, continue to stand.*

*Stand therefore, having fastened around your waist with the Belt of Truth, having put on the Breastplate of Righteousness, and having shod your feet with the Preparation of the Gospel of Peace; above all, taking the Shield of Faith, with which you will be able to quench all the fiery arrows of the Evil One. And take the Helmet of Salvation, and* **the Sword of The Spirit, which is the Word of GOD; praying at all times in the Spirit,** *with all prayer and supplication, being watchful unto this, with all perseverance and supplication for all the Believers – and also for me, that I may be given divine utterance to open my mouth boldly and make known the Mystery of the Gospel, for which I am an Ambassador, but in chains; that in it I may speak boldly, as it is necessary for me to speak.*

*Philippians 1:19-20*

*For I know that* **through your prayer, and the provision of The Spirit by Jesus, the Messiah, this will turn out for my deliverance,** *according to my earnest expectation and hope that in nothing I shall be ashamed, but with all boldness, as always, so now also the Messiah will be magnified in my body, whether by life or by death.*

## 1 Thessalonians 1:1-7

*Paul, Silas and Timothy, to the Church of the Thessalonians in God the Father and the Lord Jesus, the Messiah: Grace and Peace to you.*

*We always give thanks to GOD for all of you and continually mention you in our prayers. We remember your work of Faith, your labor prompted by love, and your endurance by Hope in our Lord Jesus, the Messiah, before our God and Father. Remember, brothers and sisters loved by GOD, that **you have been chosen because our Gospel came to you, not simply with words but also <u>with Power, with the Holy Spirit and full assurance</u>**, just as you know how we lived among you for your sake. Therefore, **you became followers of us and of the Lord, for you welcomed the message even in the middle of severe persecution, but with <u>the Joy given by the Holy Spirit</u>, so that <u>you became a great example to all the Believers</u>** in Macedonia and Achaia.*

## Titus 3:1-7

*Remind them to be compliant to rulers and authorities* (government leaders, in the Natural), *to be obedient, to be ready for every good work, to speak evil of no one, to avoid arguing, to be gentle, and to show humility toward all people. For we ourselves were once foolish, disobedient, led astray, slaves to various passions and pleasures, passing our days in malice and envy, hated by others and hating one another. **But when the goodness and loving kindness of GOD our Savior appeared, He saved us, not because of works done by us in righteousness, but according to His own Mercy, <u>by the washing of regeneration and renewal of the Holy Spirit</u>, whom He poured out on us richly through Christ Jesus our Savior, so that being justified by His Grace we might become heirs according to the Hope of Eternal Life.***

# CHAPTER FIFTEEN

# SPIRITUAL WARFARE

I will be going over some background information regarding several essential topics that are involved in Spiritual Warfare. It is critical to understand these fundamentals in order to be successful in this arena.

The topics I will be reviewing are:

1. Who We Are in the Kingdom of Heaven...
2. Who The Enemy Is & Where They Came From...
3. How We Can Fight Them...
4. Strategies For Victory...

This necessary background information is intended to ensure you will be able to come to a better understanding of why Spiritual Warfare is so critical for us all to properly operate in our Calling and in the Gifts of the Holy Spirit, and to Walk the path that GOD has set before us. It will also give you the tools you need to live a life in victory and not live in defeat.

*Revelation 1:4-6*
*John, **to the Seven Churches** (all the Churches): Grace to you and Peace **from Him** (the Father) who is and who was and who is to come, and **from the Seven Spirits** (the Holy Spirit) who are before His Throne, and **from Jesus Christ** (the Son), the faithful witness, the Firstborn from the dead, and the ruler over the kings of the Earth. **To Him** (Jesus) **who loved us and <u>washed us from our sins in His own Blood</u>, and <u>has made us Royalty</u>,** priests to His God and Father, to Him be Glory and dominion forever and ever.*

# WHO WE ARE IN THE KINGDOM OF HEAVEN

As Believers… We are Children of the Kingdom of GOD! When we were Born-Again… we entered into a War that has been raging on for Millenia. You picked a side! Because of this action, you became "known" to the evil enemy of this world, and will be targeted for attack. So, who is called to fight in this War? All of us! They will attack you regardless of whether or not you are ready or even willing to fight.

Jesus has given us the Authority to have victory over all of the strategies of the enemy. That concept is so prevalent throughout all of the New Testament, about us having Authority and Victory, and our being more than Conquerors because of what Jesus did for us. He defeated the enemy over all that is, and what was done to us before.

One thing that has helped me to get a clearer understanding of who The LORD GOD is (the Triune GOD… meaning the Father, the Son, and the Holy Spirit) and *who we are to Them*, is to reflect upon a story that originally came to me in the form of a Vision.

The following story is that Vision… which came to me in the most vivid details, colors, and emotions. I would like you to try and imagine this story in your mind as you read through it… but most importantly, that *this story is about you*…

As a young child, you suddenly find yourself walking through the forest of the most beautiful Kingdom you have ever seen, or even imagined could exist. Majestic mountains, green trees, endless colors of all types of flowers and birds, crystal clear streams of water flowing throughout the entire Kingdom, but seemingly coming from one direction, one Source. You walk towards the Source of the waters and come across the most incredible sight you have ever seen. There in the middle of this beautiful Paradise was a massive Castle. Now, this Castle is unlike anything you have ever seen or heard could even exist, and is so large that you cannot see the ends of it. As you walk towards one of its many gates, it opens for you on its own, as if it had been commanded to do so.

You walk inside, and everything you see has incredible designs and almost surreal architecture, and you wonder who could have designed and built such a place. As you continue to walk deeper and deeper inside, closer to the center, you see a grand Royal Palace in the middle of the Castle. You walk towards one of its jewel-covered doors, and as you look around, you are in awe of all you see, and yet again, the door opens on its own.

As you walk inside, you see hundreds of Ambassadors and Leaders from many Nations. They turn to see who just came through the door, as they all seem to see you at once. They all just stop speaking suddenly, then immediately begin to clear a path for you to the center of the room. As they move out of the way, you are amazed as you see three Regal Thrones, and sitting on them is the King, the Queen, and the Prince. Their eyes are fixed on you, and They all smile and open Their arms, gesturing for you to come to Them. As you slowly walk forward, you finally get close enough to Them, that the King and Queen grab you, lift you up in Their arms, place you on Their laps and say to you, "Welcome home My Child! We know that all this is new to you, and can be a little confusing, but you see, now that you have acknowledged Our Son, the Prince, as the One you are loyal to, you have become reborn into Our Kingdom and adopted as Our Child. You are now a joint heir to a royal inheritance and will be able to come to see us any time you wish. We will always be here for you, to love you, guide you, protect you, and care for you. We will teach you how to rule and exercise the Authority that We have granted you, which you now possess as Our Child. We will never leave you, and will always watch over you. You see, We have given Our Son, the Prince, to rule and be the King of kings and Lord of lords over the Earth and the Heavens above it. He has made a great sacrifice that you might live; no longer being subject to the Evil Ones of the Earth, but having Authority over them, since you are now royalty, being Our Child."

Then the King says, "We know that you will have many questions about how to walk in your new role as Our Child, and because the Prince knew He would have to return after His sacrifice, He asked Me to Promise to send the Queen to care for you all, which I have Promised Him. So, I have asked the Queen to go to the Earth and teach all of Our adopted Children everything you need to know about who Our Son the Prince is, what He has done for you, and about being royalty. She will also give you access to come to sit with Us at any time; We will hold you, love you, and teach you all you need to know. You have been granted access to Us any time you need to come to see Us. All those around Us will stop speaking, move out of the way, so you can come to the Throne any time you need to see Us. You are now royalty, one of Our Children, a prince or princess of the King, and the Queen will teach you how to walk in the Authority of the Prince, for He has been given dominion throughout all the Heavens and the Earth."

I genuinely love this story I was shown because it gives such a clear illustration of the relationship that we have with our sovereign LORD GOD, and shows us plainly that the Kingdom of GOD is a true Monarchy. The King is our Father God, the Queen is our Mother God (*the Holy Spirit*), and the Prince is our Lord Jesus – who is our "*Lord*" because He has been given dominion and rule over the Heavens and the Earth by His Father, ever since He took back control over what Adam and Eve had given away to the Evil Ones. Once we accept the Gift and Sacrifice that Their Son Jesus made, dying in our place, and providing us with a Pardon for our crimes against GOD, we become Born-Again into our new life as a legitimate Child of GOD, and are adopted in by the Royal Family. Our Heavenly Parents have a love for us that is always there.

Do you remember earlier I shared that we are given the Power to exercise the Authority that we have been granted? In the name of Jesus, and with the Power of the Holy Spirit, we can cast out the Evil Ones (*Demons*) from others and from our own lives, break curses, repel witchcraft, and not only fight off their attacks, but also advance and take back territory they once held. We are given one "Offensive" weapon, "*the Sword of The Spirit*", but the other pieces of the "*Complete Armor of GOD*" are for "Defensive" purposes. The Holy Spirit gives us the Power to fight for the Kingdom of GOD in the name of Their Son Jesus, by the Authority granted to us. We have been given a Royal Decree, signed and sealed by the King. This means that whatever we speak, the Evil Ones must comply with it, because it is not only us who speaks, but we speak as though the King Himself were speaking. We have the entire Army of the Kingdom of GOD standing behind us, and behind those words of ours that we have declared. This is because we are a Child of the King, once we become Born-Again into Their Kingdom, and as a prince or princess, our words carry Power behind them. Never forget who you are!

The Holy Spirit will teach you how and when to fight in order to be victorious. Do not allow the Evil Ones to convince you that you are weak. They can only succeed if they convince you that you are helpless and that they are powerful and should be feared. It is, in all actuality, quite the opposite, really!

Here are just a few Scriptures dealing with this topic:

*Mark 16:17*
Jesus speaking: *"And these Signs will accompany those who Believe: **In My name, they will drive out Demons; they will speak in new Tongues."***

*Luke 9:1-2*
*When Jesus had called the Twelve Apostles together, **He gave them Power and Authority to drive out all Demons and to cure diseases, and He sent them out to proclaim the Kingdom of GOD and to Heal the sick.***

*Luke 10:19*
Jesus speaking: *"**I have given you Authority** to trample on serpents and scorpions and **to overcome all the power of the enemy**; nothing will harm you."*

Try and keep these Scriptures in mind, and remember this Quote:

*"Evil thrives, where good men do nothing."*

Let's now switch gears and take a closer look at the Enemy...

Satan and his Demons were all once Angels of various Types, Levels, and Roles, and because GOD has given all of us, including them, "Free-Will", one-third of them chose to rebel against GOD and became Evil. Paul wrote a great deal about this dark side for us.

*Ephesians 6:12*
**For we do not wrestle against flesh and blood, but against <u>Principalities</u>, against <u>Powers</u>, against the <u>Rulers</u> of the darkness of this world, against the <u>Evil Spirits</u> of wickedness in the realms of the Heavens.**

Most people miss a large portion of what Paul is trying to communicate to us here, which is that those four specific descriptions (Principalities, Powers, Rulers, and Spiritual Hosts) are the "Rank" of the Demons. You see, Demons have a Rank within a Military Command Hierarchy, in the same way that an Admiral, General, Captain, and Soldiers are for our Military. This Command Hierarchy is also the same with Angels, and there are different Types and Ranks as well, like Archangels, Seraphim, Cherubim, and Guardian Angels. And both of these are very similar to the Human Military Command Hierarchy that we know today.

Their Sizes are also different, usually matching their Ranks, and will frequently match their region as well, like Country, State, City, Homes, Families. Do you recall reading in the Book of Daniel where it showed us that the Angel Gabriel was prevented from delivering a message to Daniel for 21 days when he was held captive and outnumbered by several high-ranking Regional Demons?

*Daniel 10:13*

The Angel Gabriel speaking: *"But **the prince of the kingdom of Persia** blocked me twenty-one days; and behold, **Michael, one of the chief princes** (Archangels) came to help me, for I had been left alone there with **the kings of Persia.**"*

Their Roles are also different; for example, like the spirit of Infirmity & Disease, the spirit of Fear, Anger, Addiction, Suicide, Depression, Insecurity, Weariness, etc. Many of these spirits are mentioned throughout the Bible. But, the main point to this is to understand that they have Roles; they have a job to do, just like in the Military. If you think about it in that way, it will be helpful for you to better understand your Enemy.

These Types, Sizes, and Roles can be known by someone with the Gift from the Holy Spirit called *"Discerning of Spirits"*. When the Gift of Discerning of Spirits starts to manifest in someone, they will likely start to see Dark Shadows, which are Demons, but they will also see outlines or flashes of Light, which are the Angels. Not everyone has this Gift, and it is usually directed at someone who has the Calling in an Office that deals with that specific area, like Deliverance or an Intercessor. As the Gift gets stronger, more precise details are known about who you are dealing with, like what Type of Demon it is, what it is there for, what its strategy is, how big it is, how powerful it is, and how many there are.

In addition to seeing them, there are times when a smell is associated with the Demon, usually like Sulfur or Sewage. My wife, Rowena, can smell and feel them, but less frequently, she will see them. For me, I can see and feel them, but less frequently, I will also smell them. We all are different, just like siblings in the same family can be quite different. Not everyone will manifest their Giftings and abilities in the same way. Some people may never experience any of

134

these particular Giftings dealing with the Demonic, mainly because their Calling does not have to deal with that area specifically. But, even if you are not called to a Deliverance or Intercessor Office, there are many times that a person has such a high Calling within another Office, that they will often be seriously attacked by the Demonic and will need this Discernment and Giftings to successfully fight them off.

On a more positive note, someone with these same Gifts involving Discerning of Spirits, or even someone without a Deliverance Calling, will also be able to sense the Divine side in an incredibly unique way. They will pick up smells of Roses, or fragrant Flowers, or Sweet Spices that are usually associated with the presence of the Holy Spirit or Angels. This aroma is typically accompanied by some other spiritual indication of Their presence.

*Fair warning:* Paul wanted us to understand something that we truly need to consider. Interestingly, Paul writes this warning to us in 2 Corinthians about Preachers that appear good, but, in actually are evil, then he shares something fascinating… that Satan disguises himself as an *"Angel of light"* to deceive us. That is truly astonishing, but sounds vaguely familiar, right? Well, based on the messages received during the "appearances", I have come to believe that this sounds quite a lot like the "Mary Apparitions" we have heard about over the years. This is something to certainly consider…

*2 Corinthians 11:13-15*
*For such men are false apostles, deceitful workers,*
*disguising themselves as apostles of Christ. **No wonder,**
**for even Satan disguises himself as an Angel of light.***
*Therefore, it is not surprising if his servants also disguise*
*themselves as servants of righteousness, whose end will be*
*according to their deeds.*

"The Eyes are the Window to the Soul." I have personally experienced something unusual many times before... People who are Demon-Possessed will freak out when I look them in their eyes. This can happen when you are a person who is *"Walking in the Spirit"*, and can *"see in the Spirit"*, so the Demon inside that person will realize that you can see it, and cause that person to freak out and run away, because the Demons really prefer to stay hidden within them. This has actually happened to me with Homeless people, random people on the streets, people in a Mall, or even in cars while driving.

Do Not Fear Them! I know we have all been well-trained and conditioned to fear all Demons, as we have seen in the movies we watch, the books we read, and the stories we hear about Lucifer, Satan, the Devil, or Demons.

### *2 Timothy 1:7*
### *GOD has not given us a spirit of fear, but a Spirit of Power and of Love and of Self-Control.*

Do you remember hearing that phrase before? Well, these evil things are nothing compared to GOD, who is inside you! We are not to worry about them, and we should most definitely not be afraid of them! They are not like you see them portrayed in the movies; they are *absolutely not* all-powerful, all-knowing, and so strong that they wipe out anyone who gets in their way. In the movies, typically the Christians are the ones who are killed by the Demons because "they are just so weak" and "the Demons are too strong". But that is just not reality, in fact, it is very much the exact opposite! You are very powerful, especially when you understand who you are... that you are a Child of the King, and you have been given the Authority over them!

One of the things I like to share with people, for them to better understand this concept, is this example: Have you ever seen a movie where a King gives someone a document signed by the King? He signs it, rolls it up, puts a wax seal on it, and then stamps it with his Signet Ring to prove it is genuinely from the King. The King then tells that person to go somewhere in his Kingdom and speak for him, using the King's Authority. So, the person goes on his journey to the location he was told to go by the King. He opens the scroll and reads the Commands of the King out loud. Now everyone is fearful of violating the words of the King, but the person he sent is the one reading the Commands. They are not afraid of the one speaking the words, but _they are_ fearful of the King and his Army. So, they listen and obey the one who is speaking the King's words out loud. This is very similar to how it works with us, if you know who you are, and you are operating in that same Authority that we were given by Jesus, declaring His Commands, in the name of Jesus. So, you speak to the Demons… and they must listen and obey! Simple concept, but you would be amazed at how many people do not know who they truly are in the Kingdom, even after they are Born-Again.

Something that most people are also unaware of, is that technically, the word "Satan" is actually a Title. In the Book of Enoch, it describes several "Satans", meaning more than one. It is a Title, as in a Rank or job category, meaning "The Adversary". But with that said, there is one Leader, and his name was Lucifer, but he is also called "The Devil", because of his role after he fell; not "a devil", but "The Devil", so you understand who you are dealing with. The Devil, who is "a Satan", is not everywhere, he is a singular entity that can only be at one place at a time. When he goes somewhere, he is nowhere else, and he does not know what is happening anywhere else, _until_ he gets informed by one of his cohorts of Demons. In sharp contrast to the Devil… GOD is Everywhere, Knows Everything, and is All-Powerful… and, if you are a Believer… GOD is within you.

The Devil likes people to *think* he knows everything, is so very powerful, and is everywhere, but he is not, he is pretending, because it is his nature that he is a liar.

### John 8:44

Jesus speaking: *"You are of your father **the Devil**, and you want to do the desires of your father. He was a murderer from the beginning, and does not stand in the truth because there is no truth in him. **Whenever he speaks a lie, he speaks from his own nature, for he is a liar and the father of lies."***

### 1 John 2:22

***Who is a liar, but he who denies that Jesus is the Messiah?*** *He is an antichrist who denies the Father and the Son.*

### 1 John 4:1-3

*Beloved, do not believe every spirit, but **Test the spirits** to see whether they are from GOD, because many false prophets have gone out into the world. By this, you know the Spirit of GOD: **Every spirit that confesses that Jesus is the Messiah, and has come in the flesh, is from GOD, and every spirit that does not confess Jesus, the Messiah, has come in the flesh, is not from GOD.***

"*Testing the spirits*" that you may hear from is very important for you to understand if you should listen to them, or fight them. I have had the experience many times that these Demons will speak to me, and I know many others who have had the same experience. Sometimes, there may be someone claiming to be from GOD, or speaking for GOD, so their messages must be tested.

I suggest you ask them these questions: "Who is Jesus to you?", "How do you feel about the Blood of Jesus?", "Who do you serve?", "Did Jesus come in the flesh?", and "Was Jesus the Son of God before He came in the flesh?" These questions will get a response, positive or negative, and will make their allegiance clear.

With that in mind, Psychics & Mediums claim to be given information from "God", the spirit world, a dead relative, or from their own abilities, but in actuality, it is from a "Familiar Spirit", which some call a "Family Spirit", but it is definitely _not_ from GOD. These Familiar Spirits have been around, listening, and observing, because they have been assigned to your family, as I briefly stated on page 133. For example, imagine one of these invisible Entities have observed and listened to your Grandparents for many years, but they later passed away. Then, one day, you decide to go to a Psychic or Medium, and amazingly, one of your "deceased Grandparents" talks to you through this Psychic or Medium. So, because this information they tell you is accurate private family details, you are deceived into listening to their directions. This advice will then cause you to walk contrary to GOD's Will, and follow the direction of the evil Familiar Spirit, who truly wants you to turn away from GOD, and from GOD's Will for your life. The other downside to this visit is that it will also cause an Open Door for you to be tormented "Legally" by Demons, even if you are a Child of GOD, because you are violating one of GOD's Commands not to go to a Psychic or Medium in the first place.

*Leviticus 19:31*
**"Do not turn to Mediums, or seek out Spiritists, for they will defile you. I am the LORD your GOD."**

*Leviticus 20:6-8, 26-27*
The LORD GOD speaking:  *"I will set My face against anyone who goes to Mediums and Spiritists, who commit spiritual prostitution by following them, and I will cut them off from their people.*  Consecrate yourselves and be holy, because I am the LORD your GOD.  Keep My Commands and follow them.  I am the LORD, who makes you holy.  You are to be holy to Me because I, the LORD, am Holy, and I have set you apart from the Nations to be My own.  *A man or woman who is a Medium or Spiritist among you, must be put to death.*  You are to stone them; their blood will be on their own heads."  (This shows you how much the LORD hates this!)

*Deuteronomy 18:10-12*
**There shall not be found among you anyone who practices Fortune-Telling, or uses Sorcery, or Interprets Signs, or engages in Witchcraft, or Casts Spells, or functions as Mediums or Psychics, or calls forth the Spirits of the Dead.  Anyone who does these things is an Abomination to the LORD.**

These "Open Doors" I mentioned earlier are caused by our participating with: Psychics, Mediums, Astrology, Horoscopes, Tarot Cards, Ouija Boards, Spiritism, and Pagan Rituals like Wiccan, Masonic, or other Rituals, and yes, even the "spiritual meditations" of Yoga; and *no*, I'm not talking about stretching. Additionally, "Open Doors" can be caused Naturally, as in Traumatic Events like death, illness, or violence, also Anger, Rage, Pornography, Drug Use, and even Pride or Arrogance can also cause Open Doors.

Now, what do I mean by "Pride" or "Arrogance" because that seems unusual, right?  Here is a Scripture Verse that most people don't think about often, where Solomon wrote this:

*These six things **the LORD hates**, yes, seven are an*
***abomination to GOD:** A prideful look… A lying tongue…*
*Hands that shed innocent blood… A heart that schemes*
*wicked plans… Feet that are quick to run to evil… A false*
*witness who speaks lies… And **one who spreads strife***
***among Believers.***"

Wow!  There are several things mentioned that many of us are guilty of doing.  But, if we do them, we open ourselves up to Torment, because they are things the LORD, in fact, truly "*__hates__*".  Let me give you a specific example from the New Testament:

*Luke 22:24,31-33*
*Now there was also a dispute among the Apostles, as to*
***which of them should be considered the greatest.** (Pride)*
*And the Lord said, "Simon, Simon!  Indeed, **Satan has***
***asked for you, that he may sift you as wheat.  But I have***
***prayed for you, that your faith should not fail**"* (that
sounds good so far right?  But then Jesus says,) *"and **when***
***you have returned to Me**, strengthen your brothers and*
*sisters."  But Peter said to Jesus, "**Lord, I am ready to go***
***with You, both to prison and to death.**"* (Arrogance)

Later on, we will read that Peter denied Jesus three times.

Peter made Prideful, Arrogant statements, which opened the door "Legally" for the enemy to come in and Torment him.  And you notice that Jesus *__did not__* say, *"Don't worry Peter, I won't let him come to Torment you."*  Jesus made it very clear that Peter had opened the door, and basically told him, *"When you are on the other side of this Testing, come back to Me."* Jesus clearly did not say He was going to stop it! Think about that for a moment. This type of Prideful, Arrogant statement and behavior can Open Doors… Legally… just in the same way as all the other things can, that were mentioned earlier. Be very careful what you say!

Now, some people worry that as Christian Believers, we can actually be *Possessed,* meaning Demons living inside of us. The Scriptures give us examples of people being Possessed with as many as 10,000 Demons, and this was on the inside. It is not the case for Believers, because the Holy Spirit fills the "Empty Place" on the inside of you, but only after you become Born-Again. You see, when you are Born-Again, the Holy Spirit comes into you, to fill the "Empty Place" inside you that GOD designed for the Holy Spirit to occupy, but this is also the same space that Demons *could* go into, but *only if* you are *not* Born-Again. Matthew 12:43-45 states that if you sweep the house clean, but don't fill it, then seven even more wicked Demons will come in, and the person will be worse off than before. What that is referring to is *us*, we are the house, since we are the *"Temple of the Holy Spirit"*; we are the Home where the Holy Spirit resides, so a person can *only* be Possessed *if* the Holy Spirit is *not* already there. However, we as Born-Again Believers, can be *Oppressed*. See the difference in those words? Unbelievers can be "Possessed" on the inside, but Believers can only be "Oppressed" from the outside. As it says in Luke 4:18 that Jesus came *"to set free those who are Oppressed"*. But, this doesn't mean that the oppression won't be difficult; it can be very difficult and very tormenting, with really bad voices, negative feelings of despair, and possibly some or all the emotions from the spirits I mentioned earlier on page 134. These spirits have Roles, and they perform them readily, especially if we open the door for them to attack us Legally, and don't deal with them appropriately.

Many of you may have experienced the consequences of this, and never understood it. But, there is something spiritual created when we have shared traumatic or violent experiences, or we have created Open Doors in a particular area. What is formed is called a "Soul-Tie". However, the most common way that these Soul-Ties are created is through Sexual Sin, because Sex is intended for marriage to join two Souls as one, which in actuality, is a "Godly Soul-Tie". We read clearly in 1 Corinthians 6:9-20 (later on pages 220-221) that in a Marriage, "*The two shall become one*". That phrase is what this topic is referring to; two Souls become tied together as one, through the act of having Sex. This act is fundamentally essential to connect a Married Couple. So important that a phrase is used to describe the first time the couple is joined together this way in a new Marriage is: "To Consummate a Marriage". However, a lifelong problem can develop because casual Sex is not intended for outside of a Marriage, since it still creates a Soul-Tie, only now, it is then most commonly referred to as an "Unholy or Ungodly Soul-Tie". This type of Soul-Tie can carry over into a more significant future relationship; the one that GOD ordained for you. This Ungodly Soul-Tie can interfere with and hinder you from becoming "One" with your "Soul-Mate" because you will carry this "Baggage" with you into your Marriage.

Any Soul-Tie that was not formed by a Godly Union in Marriage, between a man and a woman, must be broken off, or it will continue on into the more important relationship in your Marriage.

This information I am sharing with you is not meant to be condemning, but is meant to set you free. As it says in Romans 8:1, "*there is no condemnation for those who belong to Christ Jesus*" But, those of you who are currently doing this need to Repent, ask for Forgiveness, and get right with GOD to break these Ungodly Soul-Ties, in Jesus' name, so you will be free to meet up with your true

"Soul-Mate" that GOD has ordained for you. You also need to break any Soul-Ties which were caused by Trauma or Violence.

For those of you who have never heard the true meaning of the word "Repent"; it does not explicitly mean to turn 180 degrees around and go the opposite direction, as many say. It actually means to "Return to the Top!" If you break down the word Repent into "Re" and "Pent" you can see more clearly that "Re" is as in "Return" and "Pent" is as in a "Penthouse" which is at the "Top" of a building.

So, to "Repent" means to Return your behavior to the Top. It means to return to doing things GOD's Way, and not the way of the world, your Flesh, or the enemy. It means you take the "*High-Road*" and not the "*Low-Road*". It means you enter the "*Narrow Gate*" and not the "*Wide Gate*", where most everyone else travels. It means listening to the figurative Angel on your right shoulder (*your spirit*) and not the figurative Devil on your left shoulder (*your Flesh*). It means reading the Word of GOD instead of doing what your Flesh wants you to do instead. You get the general idea.

That change, or Return to the Top, is different for everyone because our situations are different, and what gets us in trouble may be different. But, the solution is always the same...

*Matthew 6:33*
*"Seek first the Kingdom of GOD and Righteousness, and all these things shall be given to you."*

If you "feel prompted", or as some call it, "feel convicted" about some aspect of your life that needs your attention, then ask the Holy Spirit to share with you what change is required, and how you can Return to the Ways of GOD. GOD is knocking at the door to your heart and wants to be the only One you put first.

# How We Can Fight Them

The basic concept behind Spiritual Warfare is an incredibly simple one to learn. I once taught a 3-year-old boy to fight, who was terrified and being tormented every night by these horrific Demons. His parents didn't know what to do because they were not Born-Again yet, so they were all desperate for help. When I first heard about this, I decided to pull the 3-year-old boy aside and tell him directly what he needed to do. It was only the very basics because with a child this young, you can't go into a lot of detail. So, I simply told him, "Next time you see one, you just say to them, 'In the name of Jesus, Get Out!' that's all, and they will have to leave."

So, the next time I saw him, he was so excited and ran up and hugged me and said, "I said it, they listened, and they ran out!" The concept is simple, it is really not difficult when you know who you are in the Kingdom. That child had a simple faith! He believed it, and after that, he just knew it, and was never tormented again. All these children that have "Night Terrors", or some other interpretation, because their parents are just told stories that this is normal for kids to scream and cry and go through, but it is not! Small children, and most animals, commonly see Demons much easier than adults. So, the next time a small child says they saw something, don't try and convince them that it's just their imagination, or that they are just making it up... you pray for them, you pray against it, and fight these Entities tormenting the child. Go into their room and pray; maybe it is right there, and you might see it or feel it for yourselves, so you can deal with it yourself. And, if the child is old enough, you teach them how to get rid of these Demons for themselves. GOD honors faith, especially from little children.

Although the basics are simple, and all Believers are supposed to fight any enemy that comes against us, being an "Intercessor" or being a "Warrior" with a "Deliverance Ministry" as a Calling is a much different Office. These Callings are vastly different, so I don't want you to just think that anyone should go out there and "Cast Out Demons from Possessed people", unless you are "Sent" by GOD. This is something that only these specific people who are directly called to a Deliverance Ministry should be doing. These Intercessors are also the ones who should always be praying for the Pastor, or Guest Speakers, while a message is being shared to the Believers. This is to keep them from being attacked while speaking, by placing a Hedge of Protection around those speaking and hearing the message, so the message is not hindered or stolen. Do you remember the "Parable of the Sower" that Jesus told?

*Luke 8:4-15*
*And when a great multitude had gathered, and they had come to Him from every city, Jesus spoke by a Parable: "A Sower went out to sow his seed. And as he sowed, **some fell by the wayside; and it was trampled down, and the birds of the air devoured it.** Some fell on rock; and as soon as it sprang up, it withered away because it lacked water. And some fell among thorns, and the thorns sprang up with it and choked it. **But others fell on good ground, sprang up, and yielded a crop a hundredfold."** When He had said these things, He cried out, "He who has ears to hear, let him hear!" Then His Disciples asked Him, saying, "What does this Parable mean?" And He said, "**To you, it has been given to know the Mysteries of the Kingdom of GOD**, but to the rest, it is given in Parables, that 'Seeing they may not see, and hearing they may not understand.' Now the Parable is this: The seed is the Word of GOD. **Those by the wayside are the ones who hear; then the Devil comes***

146

*and takes away the Word out of their hearts, lest they should believe and be saved. And the ones on the rock are those who, when they hear the Word, receive it with Joy. But because these have no roots, they believe for a while, and in time of Testing, they fall away. Now the ones that fell among thorns are those who, when they have heard, go out and are choked with cares, riches, and pleasures of life, and bring no fruit to maturity.* **But the ones that fell on the good ground are those who, having heard the Word with a noble and good heart, keep it and bear fruit with endurance."**

Jesus plainly shows us in this Parable that there is a Strategy of the Evil Ones to stop us from truly receiving a Word that will help us grow as a Believer, and deepen our relationship with GOD. They try and stop the Seed from taking root in good soil and bearing fruit in our lives. Intercessors are those who oppose these strategies of the Evil Ones to rob us, so they "Stand in the Gap", to fight for us, and protect those who need the help, those who may not even in know they need it. We will go deeper into all the "Offices" later in the Chapter called "The Gifts of the Holy Spirit".

When we are first Born-Again, we are often referred to as a "Baby Christian", which is a common term used around Believers to describe a new Christian, because our spirit was just newly born by the Holy Spirit. In 1 Peter 2:2, Peter writes: *"As newborn babies, desire the pure Milk of the Word, that you may grow..."*

I cannot emphasize this enough... we _must_ Read the Bible! The Word of GOD is food for our spirit and our Soul; even if you don't "memorize" the Scriptures, it gets in your spirit and Soul.

As Jesus said in John 14, "*The Holy Spirit will teach you all things and remind you of everything I have said to you.*" This means that She will *remind you of the Scriptures that you read*, in order to help you, or someone else, with some life situation and build up the Body of Believers. So, you don't need to try and memorize the Scriptures, but you do need to read them, to get them inside you. Reading is also very important for all of us to understand the Character of GOD, so when you hear a voice in your head, you will be able to tell whether or not that voice is your Flesh, the Holy Spirit, a Demon, an Angel, the Father, or Jesus talking to you; all of which are possible. This is to better understand the Character of each of these voices, so you know who is speaking to you, and determine who to listen to, and who to fight, so we must all read the Word of GOD. We also need to understand our own Flesh, to truly understand what we are capable of, and what our own weaknesses are, so we don't listen to our Flesh telling us to do something against the Character of GOD.

Reading the Word is not only to help us grow in our Faith, and stay strong in our spirit, but it is also to get these specific pieces of the "*Armor of GOD*", as mentioned in Ephesians 6 below, in order for us to be prepared to fight against all the strategies of the enemy.

*Ephesians 6:10-18*
*Finally, my brothers and sisters, be strong in the Lord* (Jesus) *and in the Power of His might.* ***Put on the complete Armor of GOD, that you may be able to stand against the strategies of the Devil.*** *For we do not wrestle against flesh and blood, but against Principalities, against Powers, against the Rulers of the darkness of this world, against the Evil Spirits of wickedness in the realms of the Heavens. Therefore, take up the complete Armor of GOD, that you may be able to oppose them in the evil day, and having done all things, continue to stand. Stand therefore, having fastened around your waist with*

148

*the **Belt of Truth**, having put on the **Breastplate of**
**Righteousness**, and having **Shoes** on your feet with the*
***Preparation of the Gospel of Peace***; *above all, taking the*
***Shield of Faith**, with which you will be able to quench all*
*the fiery arrows of the Evil One. And take the **Helmet of**
**Salvation**, and **the Sword of The Spirit, which is the Word**
**of GOD**; **praying at all times in the Spirit**, with all prayer*
*and supplication, being watchful unto this, with all*
*perseverance and supplication for all the Believers*

The one offensive weapon mentioned by Paul is "*the Sword
of The Spirit, which is the Word of GOD*". The "*Shoes*" that are needed
to stand and fight, is the "*Preparation of the Gospel*". The "Gospel"
means the "Good News" referring to the "Pardon" that Jesus offered;
that Free Gift of Salvation by His taking the Death Penalty for us,
shedding the precious "*Blood of Jesus*" from a perfect "*Lamb of God*"
and providing a Resurrection into Eternal Life, which is written about
in detail in the Word of GOD. Both of these components of the Armor,
the Sword and the Shoes, come from reading the Word of GOD. The
Sword of The Spirit seems like an obvious weapon to fight with, but
what about Shoes? What does that have to do with fighting? Well, if
any of you have ever stepped barefoot in rocks, you know exactly
what that is about. Now imagine, you had to fight someone, barefoot,
standing in rocks. How sturdy would you be to stand firm in your
faith and your belief and fight the enemy? You would not be very
stable in your footing at all, because your feet are not covered! The
Shoes to cover your feet will enable you to "*Stand*" firm and give you
the stabile footing you need to fight, and this only comes from reading
the Word of GOD.

*Revelation 12:11*
*And **they defeated the Devil by the Blood of the Lamb,**
**and by the Word their testimony**. And they did not love*
*their lives so much that they were afraid to die.*

*Matthew 4:1-11*

*Then Jesus was led up by The Spirit into the wilderness to be Tested by the Devil. And when He had fasted forty days and forty nights, afterward He was hungry. Now when the Tempter came to Him, he said, "If You are the Son of GOD, command that these stones become bread." But Jesus answered and said, "**It is written**, 'Man shall not live by bread alone, but by every word that proceeds from the mouth of GOD.' " Then the Devil took Him up into the Holy City, set Him on the highest point of the Temple, and said to Him, "If You are the Son of GOD, throw Yourself down. For it is written: 'He shall give His Angels charge over you,' and, 'In their hands they shall bear you up, lest you dash your foot against a stone.' " Jesus said to him, "Again, **it is written**, 'You shall not Test the LORD your GOD.' " Again, the Devil took Him up on an exceedingly high mountain, and showed Him all the kingdoms of the world and their glory. And he said to Him, "All these things I will give You if You will fall down and worship me." Then Jesus said to him, "Away with you, Satan! For **it is written**, 'You shall worship the LORD your GOD, and Him only you shall serve.' " Then the Devil left Him, and behold, Angels came and ministered to Him.*

In Matthew 4, we see that Jesus used the Word of GOD to defeat the Devil when he tried to Test Him. You notice He said a very important phrase three times… "*It Is Written*". These three times that Satan tried to Test Jesus, the answer was that He spoke Scripture back to him. So, you *must* read the Word of GOD in order to speak it back to the enemy. You also will notice that when Satan tried to use Scripture out of context, to deceive Jesus into doing what he wanted, that Jesus understood the Truth, and spoke Scripture back. The Holy Spirit will help you not only remember Scripture, but give you proper context to understand Truth, so you will not be deceived by the enemy, or by someone like a false teacher or false prophet.

We need to read the Word (*Milk*) but also become mature and grow enough to move on into the deeper things of GOD (*solid food, meat*), like "Spiritual Warfare" and "The Gifts of the Holy Spirit". In Hebrews 5 we read,

*Hebrews 5:13-14*
*"For everyone who drinks only Milk is unskilled in the Word of righteousness, for he is a Baby. But **solid food** belongs to **those who are mature**, that is, **those who by reason of practice** have **their senses exercised** to discern both good and evil."*

This means you need to exercise your spiritual senses, just like you exercise your muscles, in order to get stronger and grow mature in the things of The Spirit. So, the more you practice using your Armor, your Weapons, and your Giftings, within the context of your Office... the stronger you will become.

Before you pray and perform Spiritual Warfare, you should Anoint yourself, others, your house, or your room with Anointing Oil. This is a Biblical concept and was used in Old and New Testament times. Anointing Oil is symbolic of the Power that comes from the Holy Spirit, who is absolutely needed to fight, since these battles are not in the Natural, but are in the Spirit. The Oil in and of itself has no power, but it is a reminder that we are dependent on the Power that only comes from the Holy Spirit, to enable us to fight.

When we pray, we also must Close all Open Doors by asking forgiveness for ourselves, for others, and even for those who have committed sin or shed blood on a place. This is especially important to pray over the places we visit, like hotel rooms while traveling, since many people have stayed there before us. If you go to visit someone's house, and you feel oppression, you anoint yourself, anoint the house, and pray over it. Speak these things out loud and cancel the assignments and strategies of the enemy in your life, and speak their destruction. Plead the "*Blood of Jesus*" over that place, that it would be washed and cleansed of all evil.

I need to ensure I give you all a warning: **_Never_** lay hands on someone unless you are specifically told by the Holy Spirit to do that, since you are exposing yourself to their Demons. So, unless you are told to do it, you would be vulnerable to being attacked by their Demons. Especially, **_Do Not_** try and cast out Demons from people unless you are called to the Office of a Deliverance Ministry and specifically told to do so by the Holy Spirit. Think of it this way; you would *not* want someone to Operate on a Patient, unless they were trained and certified as a Surgeon in the Medical Field, right?

There is a really good example in the New Testament about what happened to some who tried Casting Out Demons without being told. In Acts 19, Luke writes,

### *Acts 19:13-16*
*Then some of the traveling Jewish Exorcists **took it upon themselves** to call upon the name of the Lord Jesus over those who had evil spirits, saying, "We exorcise you by the Jesus whom Paul preaches." Also, there were seven sons of Sceva, a Jewish chief priest, who also did this. And **the evil spirit answered** and said, "Jesus I know, and Paul I know; but who are you?" Then the man in whom the evil spirit was, leaped on them, overpowered them, and prevailed against them**, so that they ran out of that house naked and wounded.*

There is a vast difference between fighting the enemy that comes against you, or your family, who are being Oppressed, and you actually attempting to cast out Demons from a within a person who is Possessed. That is where the Calling of an Intercessor comes in, and the Office of a Deliverance Ministry. Unless it is your Calling or your Gifting… Do not try it unless you are told!

*Always Speak in Tongues* while in battle; you are more powerful since you are speaking the words that the Holy Spirit is declaring through you. That does not mean you cannot speak in your native language; I am only saying you also need to Speak in Tongues; this way, you provide the Holy Spirit an opportunity to speak into the situation as well. This concept is apparent in Romans 8:26-28 and in 1 Corinthians 14:2 below, as well as earlier, stated in Ephesians 6:18 (page 149), where it says that during Spiritual Warfare, we should be *"praying at all times in the Spirit"*.

*Romans 8:26-28*
*Likewise, **The Spirit also helps us in our weaknesses, for we do not know what we should pray for as we need to, but The Spirit Herself intercedes on our behalf, crying out with words that cannot be expressed.** Now searching the deepest parts of our hearts, the purpose of The Spirit is known, because the **intercession made by The Spirit for Believers is according to the Will of GOD**. And we know that **all things work together for good to those who love GOD**, to those who are the Called, according to the divine purpose.*

*1 Corinthians 14:2*
*For **he who speaks in a Tongue does not speak to men, but to GOD**, for no one understands him; however, **in the Spirit, he speaks Mysteries**.*

There is Power in the Tongue!  As it says clearly in the Book of James, always speak blessings over yourself, over your family, over others, and over your situation.  Do not speak negative, because they end up becoming curses when you say, "I'm such a…", or say "I always fail!" or "That person is such a…".  Proverbs 23:7 cautions us, *"for as a man thinks within himself, so he is"*.  James specifically warns us that we are speaking a Curse.  So, always speak Blessings!

*James 3:8-10*
*But no one can tame the Tongue; it is a restless evil and full of deadly poison.* ***With it we Bless our Lord and Father, and with it we Curse men****, who have been made in the likeness of GOD;* ***from the same mouth come both Blessing and Cursing****.  My brothers and sisters, these things ought not to be this way.*

Fasting and Prayer really does help us to be victorious over the "strong ones", in that it weakens your Flesh and strengthens your spirit.  But in general, as you practice, grow in your skills, and are faithful with what you are given, you will get promoted, so the spiritual fighting becomes easier with each successive level of your promotions.  This works in the same way for us, as I mentioned before regarding Angels and Demons, similar to being in the Military, in that they have levels.  These promotions given may include new Weapons, new Skills, better Understanding, new Strategies, or just increased Power and Strength.  In John 3 below, referring to when the Holy Spirit was poured out upon Jesus, it says the Power was given to Him without measure, meaning without limitation or level, like it is for all of us.  Jesus, even as a Man, was given it all at once.

We all start at a very low level, because as you recall, we all start as Baby Christians. You would not give the keys from a Race Car to a Toddler, because they would crash. You would give tools that proportionally match their level of maturity, and their skills and abilities as they are growing. In the same way that a person goes through School, you start in Kindergarten in Elementary School, then work your way up to Middle School, then High School, then College; as you learn and grow in the Kingdom of GOD, you are promoted, and your Power and Skills increase with each subsequent level.

*John 3:34-35*
*For Jesus, whom GOD has sent, speaks the Words of GOD,*
*for He was __not given The Spirit by measure__. The Father*
*loves the Son and has __given all things into His hand__.*

So, now let's all compare that to what it says about us as Believers, and what we are given.

*Romans 12:3*
**GOD has distributed to each one __a measure of Faith__.**

*Ephesians 4*
**But to each one of us, Grace was given according to the**
**__measure__ of Christ's Gift.**

*1 Corinthians 13:9-11*
*For __we Know in part and we Prophesy in part__. But when*
*that which is complete has come, then that which is in part*
*will be done away.* (as we become more like Jesus, who
was given the Spirit without measure) *When I was a child,*
*I spoke as a child, I understood as a child, I thought as a*
*child; but when I became a man, I put away childish things.*

Now, let's go over a few more strategies and other useful information that will be helpful for your encounters with Evil Ones, and help you navigate the world of Spiritual Warfare.

Generational Curses are curses that are passed down through many generations, usually by the Familiar Spirits assigned to our families. This means that the same types of problems run in the family; things like Diseases, Divorce, Addiction, Violence, Fear, just to name a few. They are usually created by one of our Ancestors doing something evil in the sight of the LORD that opened the door Legally for the curse to operate. They must be broken off from the individuals and the families, so they will not continue to cause damage to the family members. This concept of Generational Curses is clearly shown in many Scriptures, including the New Testament. The first time it is mentioned in Scripture is within the context of the Second of Ten Commandments. Right after the LORD tells Moses to write the First Commandment, *"I am the LORD your GOD… you shall have no other gods before Me."* then comes the Second, which states to all of us plainly,

*Exodus 20:4-6*
*"**You must not make for yourself a carved image** – any likeness of anything that is in Heaven above, or that is on the Earth beneath, or that is in the Sea; **you must not bow down to them nor worship them**. For I, the LORD your GOD, am a jealous God, who will not tolerate your affection for any other gods. **I lay the sins of the parents upon their children; the entire family is affected, even children in the third and fourth generations** of those who reject me. But I lavish My unfailing Love and Mercy for a thousand generations on those who love Me and obey My Commands."*

And again, the LORD repeated this idea a short time later to Moses when He actually visited Moses in person on Earth.

*Exodus 34:5-7*

*Then the LORD came down in a cloud and stood there with Moses; and He called out His own name, LORD. The LORD passed in front of Moses, calling out, "LORD! The LORD! The God of compassion and mercy! I am slow to anger and filled with unfailing love and faithfulness. I lavish unfailing love to a thousand generations. I forgive iniquity, rebellion, and sin. **But, I do not excuse the guilty. I lay the sins of the parents upon their children and grandchildren; the entire family is affected – even children in the third and fourth generations.**"*

*Galatians 1:6-9*

Paul speaking: *"I am shocked that you are turning away so soon from GOD, who called you to Himself through the loving mercy of the Messiah. You are following a different way that pretends to be the Gospel but is not the Gospel at all. You are being fooled by those who deliberately twist the truth concerning the Messiah.*

***Let GOD's Curse fall on anyone,** including us, or even an Angel from heaven, **who preaches a different kind of Gospel than the one we preached to you.** I say again what we have said before: If anyone preaches any other Gospel than the one you welcomed, **let that person be cursed**."*

Yes, Curses can still operate in your life, even when you are Born-Again. Do you remember what happened to Peter when he opened the door to Satan? Do not give the enemy the Legal right to enter your life and Torment you, even if it came from your Ancestors. Fight them!

Not every opportunity is from GOD, even when it looks like a good thing.  In fact, the wrong opportunity or relationship can come along for the sole purpose of taking you off GOD's path.  You always need to ask the Holy Spirit if any opportunity or relationship is truly from GOD.  We read an excellent example of this in Luke 15:11-32.  Recall what happened to the *"Prodigal Son"* who decided to do things his own way and take his own path, and just how difficult his life was until he returned to his Father.  Always get Confirmation regarding big decisions, so you don't end up going down the wrong path and walking outside the Will of GOD.  Always talk with the Holy Spirit and make sure you Confirm any plans you have, making sure they are truly GOD's Will, and not just your own.

Speak a "Hedge of Protection" around you, your family, your home, or others, forming it out of the Fire of the Holy Spirit.  Ask the LORD for Angels to stand watch around you, and your family, in order to protect you wherever you go, even in your sleep.

Speak a covering of *"The Blood of Jesus"* over all the people and homes that you are fighting for, that they are washed, cleansed, and protected from all evil.  Do you recall in Exodus 12 how the Lamb's Blood was placed on the Doorframe of the house to protect the occupants from being killed by the Destroyer?  Additionally, Jesus was called *"the Lamb of GOD that takes away the sins of the world"* in John 1:29, and He shed His Blood for us on Passover.

*1 Corinthians 5:7*
**For indeed Christ Jesus, our Passover Lamb, has been Sacrificed for us.**

*Exodus 12:21-24*
Moses speaking:  *"Pick out and take Lambs for yourselves according to your families, and **kill the Passover Lamb**. And you shall take a bunch of Hyssop, dip it in the blood*

*that is in the basin, and **apply to the top and two sides of the doorposts with the Lamb's blood** that is in the basin. And none of you shall go out of the door of his house until morning. For the LORD will pass through to strike the Egyptians; and **when He sees the blood on the doorframe, the LORD will pass over the door and not allow the Destroyer to come into your houses to strike you.** And you shall observe this thing as an ordinance for you and your ancestors forever."*

<u>Hebrews 10:10,12</u>
*For GOD's Will was for us to be sanctified by **the Sacrifice of the Body of Jesus Christ, once for all.** But **our High Priest** (Jesus) **offered Himself to God as a single Sacrifice for sins forever**, then He sat down at God's right-hand.*

Speaking the words *"The Blood of Jesus"* out loud causes Demons to tremble and run away. It harms them in ways that we can't fully comprehend; we only know it works. Each time you say the phrase, it is like stabbing them with a spiritual knife.

I highly recommend the book, *"**The Power of the Blood**"* by Whyte; as it brings a unique perspective to how we can operate in the Power and Authority that comes through the *"Blood of Jesus"*.

Don't be afraid to ask others for help when needed, because there are times when we will all need some help.

<u>Matthew 18:19-20</u>
Jesus speaking: *"Again **I say to you that if two of you agree on Earth concerning anything that they ask, it will be done for them by My Father in Heaven.** For where two or three are gathered together in My name, I am there in the midst of them."*

159

*Deuteronomy 32:30*
***"one will chase a thousand; two will chase ten thousand"***

*Genesis 2:18*
*And the LORD GOD said, "**It is not good that man should be alone**; I will make him a helper comparable to him."*

*Ecclesiastes 4:9-12*
***Two are better than one***, *because they have a good reward for their labor. For if they fall, one will lift up his companion. But woe to him who is alone when he falls, for he has no one to help him up. Again, if two lie down together, they will keep warm; but how can one be warm alone? Though **one may be overpowered by another, two can withstand him, but a threefold cord is not quickly broken**.*

When we Pray together, we are 10 times greater. Husbands and Wives praying together are 10 times stronger, which is why the enemy hates marriage and is always trying to break them up.

Single people really should find someone else to pray with them during some battles. We read that clearly in these last three Verses, which show us that they need to be just as Jesus stated in Matthew 18 (page 159), "*two or three gathered together*", and this way, Jesus will also be with them. If single people try and fight some battles alone, they are much more vulnerable to attack.

For example: Sometimes, our battle may involve Witchcraft sent from a Coven that practices their particular form of Witchcraft using the Dark Arts, or sometimes called "Black Magic". It truly is best not to fight this type of battle alone.

I wrote a "Model Prayer" for Spiritual Warfare and have shared it with others; It is meant to be helpful as a starting point for developing your own prayer. The words you use may be different for each specific circumstance, but this gives you a good starting point. In the same way that Jesus gave a Model Prayer for us to pray to the Father, this is also not meant to simply be read over and over without having an understanding of the words. It goes something like this:

"Heavenly Father, in the name of Jesus, with the Power of the Holy Spirit, and by the Authority you have given me as Your Child, I take Authority over any Demon or any evil that is coming against me, or my family. Any witchcraft or curses that have been spoken over me, or my family, and any Generational Curses from my past, I bind these Demons in chains and speak their destruction by the Fire of the Holy Spirit. I return any witchcraft, or curses spoken, back upon the head of the one speaking it. I plead the Blood of Jesus over myself, my family, and my home, and ask forgiveness for all our sins, so we are washed by the Blood of Jesus and set free from all Torments and Curses. In Jesus' name, I pray. Amen."

Some of you may have heard terms like "Bind" or "Loose" when dealing with Spiritual Warfare. This came from Matthew 16 where Jesus said, *"I will give you the keys of the Kingdom of Heaven, and whatever you **bind** on Earth will be bound in Heaven, and whatever you **loose** on Earth will be loosed in Heaven."* To Bind something means *"to tie it up"*, whereas the word Loose means *"to destroy it"*. I normally don't use the old English word "Loose" in Spiritual Warfare, because it has another meaning, which is to *"untie something"*, and that is not what I am looking to do. You can, however, use it to refer to when you are declaring a Blessing that has been hindered to be "Loosed", so it is no longer hindered.

# CHAPTER SIXTEEN

# THE GIFTS OF THE HOLY SPIRIT

## INTRODUCTION

Throughout our lives, we've seen people that we consider to be "Gifted". They seem to have been given unique Talents and Abilities even from Birth. Some people will properly acknowledge and be thankful to GOD for providing them these Gifts, but others will just take the credit for themselves, considering it their own abilities. Throughout the Old and New Testaments, the Scriptures give a very clear picture as to _where_ these Gifts truly come from… they are from the Holy Spirit.

Besides Talents in the Natural, like the Arts, Music, Technology, Mechanical Aptitude, Craftsmanship, and working with our hands, some people also have skills with Cooking, Animals, or Farming, just to name a few, although there are many more; we are also given various Spiritual Gifts and Ministries, assuming we are Believers. Most of my focus will be on the spiritual aspects of our Gifts received by the Holy Spirit, and not quite as much as on the ones in the Natural.

We, as Believers, have each been given different Functional Ministries or Offices, and we are also given Spiritual Gifts to complement it. Both are intended to be used to build up (_edify_) ourselves and other Believers, as well as draw Unbelievers to GOD. They are meant to help us, and others, navigate this life and enable us to continue to Walk forward in our relationship with GOD. They are used to prove that GOD is alive and well and within us. We also need to understand that they are given to us _in measure_ "_as The Holy Spirit Wills_", and in proportion to the level of our Faith.

But, if we are to be used by GOD in a mighty way, it comes at a cost! When I was 27 years old, my Mentor gave me a strong warning when I had pridefully mentioned to him that I wanted not only to receive Power from the Holy Spirit, but have "All the Gifts!". He warned me and said, "Be careful what you ask for!"; he then prayed and spoke a Prophetic Word over me saying, "You will receive ALL these things you have asked for, *but*... there is One Word to describe what must come first before that... 'Pain!' ". And I can tell you now that after these many years later... he was right. But...Why would this happen? Isn't GOD a Loving God? Absolutely!

Solomon, who was given so much Wisdom from the Holy Spirit, that he was considered to be the wisest man ever to have lived (*besides Jesus, of course*), wrote warnings regarding this topic in Ecclesiastes and Proverbs. We are also given a couple of examples in the New Testament as well.

*Ecclesiastes 1:18*
**For with much Wisdom, comes much sorrow; the more Knowledge, the more grief.**

*Luke 12:48*
*And the Lord Jesus said, "For everyone to whom much is given, from him much will be required; and to whom much has been entrusted, of him much more will be expected."*

*James 3:1*
*Not many of you should become Teachers, my fellow Believers, because you know that **we who Teach will be judged more strictly by GOD**.*

164

### Proverbs 17:3
**Fire Tests the purity of silver and gold, but <u>the LORD</u>
<u>Tests the heart</u>.**

When gold is refined, it must be heated with Fire until it has melted. The impurities then float to the top where they can be seen and removed. In this same way, "Testing" helps us to be able to see our impurities or "baggage", and other issues within our Souls that hinder us from Walking with GOD. We go through "Trials by Fire" or a "Wilderness Experience" to help us understand who we are, and what is hindering our Walk. This process can be very painful, but it is also very necessary to help us move into the Blessings that GOD has planned for us, plans from before we were even conceived. But besides the Past, the Future comes into play as well with this saying:

*"It's about where you're going... not about where you've been."*

In other words, sometimes, what you are going through has less to do with your past, but has much more to do with your future. These difficult things that have happened to you, and will happen to you, are because of your Calling, who you are, and where you are going, not necessarily because you committed sin. Some people think they are being punished, or some other evil thing, when in fact, it is Testing that needs to occur in order to move them forward into their Calling. Do you recall how Jesus, after He was Baptized and filled with the Holy Spirit, but before He started His public Ministry, was *"Led into the Wilderness"* to be Tested by the Devil for 40 days? Now, I know if you are just coming to realize this, it may sound crazy that the Holy Spirit *"Led"* Jesus there, but that is precisely what happened. Those Wilderness Experiences, like happened to Moses, John the Baptist, and others, also happen to us; these Trials by Fire are necessary for our growth. More on "Trials" later in Chapter 18.

One of the things we need, in order for us to be properly guided by the Holy Spirit, is to have an understanding of the "Logos Word" and a "Rhema Word". So, what is the difference between the Greek words "Logos" and "Rhema"? Logos is the written Word (Bible) and Rhema is the *"Living Word"* from the Holy Spirit. An example of this would be if I said to you, "I was reading the Bible (Logos) when the Holy Spirit spoke to me and gave me a Word (Rhema) which provided me a fresh perspective and understanding of what I was reading." Another example would be: The Pharisees knew the written Word (Logos) very well, but Jesus had a great deal of trouble with them because they did not know the Living Word (Rhema), which is the Spirit of the Word, provided by the Holy Spirit, so they had no real understanding of its true meaning.

*1 Peter 1:22-25*
***Since you have purified your Souls by obeying the Truth through <u>The Spirit</u> in genuine Love of the brothers and sisters, Love one another sincerely with a pure heart, since you have been Born-Again, not of perishable seed but imperishable, through <u>the Living Word of GOD which resides in us</u>, because, "All flesh is as grass, and all its glory is as the flower of the grass. The grass withers and its flower falls away, but the Word of the LORD endures forever." But this is the <u>Living Word</u> which by the Gospel was preached to you.***

Do you recall when Jesus spoke of our future, referring to us as future Believers, saying in John 14 about us?

*John 14:12*
*"Truly, truly, I say to you, <u>whoever believes in Me will also do the Works that I do; and even Greater Works than these will they do</u>, because I am going to the Father."*

Well, the *"Greater Works"* part we will do, hasn't happened yet, but it will happen soon. The outpouring of the Holy Spirit mentioned in Joel 2:28-32 is coming soon. GOD is about to step up and show the world They are alive and in control. So, we all need to make room for the Holy Spirit to move in a fresh New Anointing. <u>*Do Not*</u> put Her in a box! We cannot make the mistake of allowing our expectations, or our Traditions, to interfere with GOD's Truth. We cannot confine GOD to a box, and place limitations on a Limitless, Infinite, All-Powerful God. We cannot, if we expect to be part of the outpouring and Revival that is coming. We all need a fresh Rhema Word in our lives to guide us into that future.

Also, don't make the common mistake of copying another person's Anointing! I've seen this done so many times before, where someone will see a Pastor or Preacher or Prophet, and the person will just copy them hoping to get the same thing. That was theirs, but you need to have your own Anointing. GOD wants to do something new and unique, not what has already been done. So, you *<u>do not</u>* want to just copy someone else, but especially not if you would like to have a fresh new filling of the Holy Spirit.

Revival… Global Revival is coming!

Be Ready!

# WHAT ARE THE OFFICES OR MINISTRIES ?

What are the Offices or Ministries of the Holy Spirit that are mentioned in the Bible?  Well, there are many!  The list below I am providing covers the majority of them, but it is not meant to be exclusive.

Ministries / Offices:
- **Apostles** – are Ambassadors to Jesus; one who helps Believers start or grow Churches by proving leadership and direction and vision for a Church.

- **Prophets** – one who is a mouthpiece for GOD, speaks as if GOD were speaking out loud, and is very accurate.  This differs from the Gift of Prophecy, which others can have.

- **Teachers** – are Master Instructors regarding the things of GOD and are able to help people navigate through life.

- **Workers of Miracles** – is one who performs Miracles that only GOD could do, in order to prove GOD is real.

- **Healers** – are one who cures the body of sickness or disease, both Naturally and Supernaturally.

- **Pastors** – are one who shepherds, guides, oversees, and protects the Children of GOD.

- **Evangelists** – are one who spreads the Gospel of Salvation that we have through Faith in Jesus as our Messiah and Lord.

- **Preachers** – are one who speaks Divine Truth to others, including new Revelations.

- **Deliverance**– is one who is called to Cast out Demons from people, objects, and places, as well as break Curses and Soul-Ties off of others.

- **Intercessor** – is one who prays or intercedes to GOD on behalf of others; those who stand in the middle, between the person and evil, and oppose the Evil Ones for others.

- **Praise & Worship** – is one who plays music or sings songs to GOD, and will encourage others to do the same; they will worship GOD and help others to worship GOD as well.

- **Administrations** – is one who performs governing or support roles for others in Office, like in Management, Finance, Audio, Video, Childcare, Janitorial, etc.

- **Helps** – is one who helps others in need with food, shelter, clothes, money, support, guidance, etc.

In Colossians 3, Paul writes to us,

### *Colossians 3:22-25*
*"Servants (Employees), obey in all things your earthly masters (Employers), not only when they see you, as men-pleasers do, but in the sincerity of heart, fearing GOD. And whatever you do, **do it heartily, as to the Lord and not to men**, knowing that from the Lord you will receive the reward of the inheritance; for you serve the Lord Jesus. But he who does wrong will be repaid for what he has done, and there is no partiality."*

What this Scripture is telling us is that when you are called into an Office or Ministry, you don't always have to be someone who works in a Church. Our Callings can be out in the corporate world, in Industry, working for a company, or running your own business, but you are making an impact for the Kingdom, by working as if you are working for Jesus. What is truly important, is what you do with it. It may be your Trade, but it also can be your Ministry, if you Witness to people, or just let others see Jesus in you, so that they will be drawn to you like a lamp, so you can then point them to Jesus.

I feel compelled to give you a Warning about Offices and Ministries. Do not take on an Office or Role, especially in a Church where you are influencing others, unless you are told directly from the Holy Spirit, and it is Confirmed by others. You will fail, and you will take others down with you. Usually, in the Office we are Called to, we have a deep passion for it within us, whatever the Calling, we are drawn to it, and have a passion for it. It is not something that you _decide_ to do intellectually, or figure out, it is simply who you are, and you know it in your heart. With some people, it is Cooking, some it may be Music or Singing, but with me, well, you would not want to taste my cooking or hear me sing, because it is just _not_ who I am. So, we are not supposed to do things we are not called to do, or we will fail, but unfortunately, I have seen this done many times.

I have seen people fill an opening just because there was an opening somewhere, even in a Church, and they take it just because it's open, and someone told them, "Hey, you should go fill that opening." so then they take it, and they fail. Why? They failed because they never asked the Holy Spirit, or got Confirmation from anyone else, whether or not they should actually be doing it. So, it doesn't matter if it is Friends, Family, or just people you have known for a long time, telling you that you or someone else should just fill an opening. No! You ask the Holy Spirit and She will tell you if you or another person are Called to this role, or you will fail. And, the worst part is that you will likely take others with you in your failure. It would be best if you asked the Holy Spirit who the right person is, because the right person for the opening might actually be someone you do not expect. But, if you really need to fill a position, in a regular job, or even one inside a Church, and if you are the decision-maker, then you need to Confirm that you choose the right person according to GOD, not yourself. And, if you are that person filling the opening somewhere, then you make sure there is a lot of Confirmation that you are truly supposed to go into it… otherwise, you will fail.

<u>Matthew 25:14-30</u>

Jesus speaking: *"For the Kingdom of Heaven is like a Man traveling to a far country, who called His own servants and delivered His goods to them.* **And to one He gave five Talents, to another two, and to another one, to each according to his own ability;** *and immediately He went on a journey. Then he who had received the five Talents went and traded with them, and made another five Talents.* (Promotion) *And likewise, he who had received two gained two more also.* (Promotion) *But he who had received one went and dug in the ground and hid his Lord's money. After a long time, the Lord of those servants came and settled accounts with them. So, he who had received five Talents came and brought five other Talents, saying, 'Lord, you delivered to me five Talents; look, I have gained five more Talents besides them.' His Lord said to him,* **'Well done, good and faithful servant; you were faithful over a few things, I will make you ruler over many things. Enter into the Joy of your Lord.'** *He also who had received two Talents came and said, 'Lord, you delivered to me two Talents; look, I have gained two more Talents besides them.' His Lord said to him, 'Well done, good and faithful servant; you have been faithful over a few things, I will make you ruler over many things. Enter into the Joy of your Lord.'* **Then he who had received the one Talent came and said, 'Lord,** *I knew You to be a hard Man, reaping where You have not sown, and gathering where You have not scattered seed. And* **I was afraid, and went and hid Your Talent in the ground.** *Look, there you have what is Yours.' But his Lord answered and said to him,* **'You wicked and lazy servant,** *you knew that I reap where I have not sown, and gather where I have not scattered seed. So,* **you ought to have deposited My money with the bankers, and at My Coming, I would have received back My own with interest.** *So, take the Talent from him, and give it to him who has ten Talents. For to everyone who has, more will be given, and he will have abundance; but* *from him who does not have, even what he has will be taken away.  And cast the unprofitable servant into the outer darkness.  **There will be weeping and gnashing of teeth**."*

The "Parable of the Talents" that Jesus just gave expresses the idea concerning Believers using their Talents (Skills, Gifts, Office) properly for GOD, or misusing them without consideration for others, or for why GOD gave them the Talent in the first place.  And, if you don't intend to help others, don't be surprised if you don't receive any, or that which was meant for you will be given to another.  GOD won't provide you with something, like a Gift designed for the use in the Body of Christ, if you have no intention of doing anything with it, except saying, "I'm saved, I'm going to Heaven, so I don't need to worry about anyone else."  Wrong!  That is _not_ what being a Christian Believer is truly all about.  GOD doesn't want to give you a light, like a Lamp, if you intend to put it under a basket… or like it says in the Parable, he buried his Talent and did not use it for others.  So, GOD judged him harshly for not using his Talent wisely for others.

We, as Believers, are all assigned one or more Offices, but will also utilize the different Gifts.  For example, Paul had multiple Offices, as he mentioned in 2 Timothy 1:11, "*I was appointed a Preacher, an Apostle, and a Teacher*", but Paul also operated in several other Offices, and many of the Gifts were given to him by the Holy Spirit.  The following Scriptures go over this in much more detail regarding the Offices we are given as Believers.

*1 Corinthians 12:18,27-31*

*But now GOD has set the <u>members</u>, each one of them, <u>in the Body</u> just as intended. Now <u>you are the Body of Christ</u>, and <u>members</u> individually. And GOD has appointed these in the Church: first <u>Apostles</u>, second <u>Prophets</u>, third <u>Teachers</u>, after that <u>Miracles</u>, then <u>Gifts of Healings</u>, <u>Helps</u>, <u>Administrations</u>, <u>varieties of Tongues</u>. Are all Apostles? Are all Prophets? Are all Teachers? Are all workers of Miracles? Do all have Gifts of Healings? Do all speak with Tongues? Do all interpret? But earnestly desire the best Gifts.*

*Romans 12:3-8*

*For I say, through the Grace given to me, to everyone who is among you… do not to think of yourselves more highly than you ought to think, but think sensibly, as GOD has distributed to each one a measure of Faith. For as we have many members in one Body, but all the members do not have the same function, so we, being many, are one Body in Christ, and <u>individually members of one another</u>. Having then Gifts differing according to the Grace that is given to us, let us use them: if Prophecy, let us Prophesy in proportion to our Faith; or Service, let us use our Faith in our Serving; whosoever teaches, in teaching; whosoever encourages, in encouragement; whosoever gives, with generosity; whosoever leads, with diligence; and whosoever shows mercy, with cheerfulness.*

*Ephesians 4:1-16*

*I, therefore, the prisoner of the Lord, urge you to <u>Walk worthy of the Calling</u> with which you were called, with all humility and gentleness, with patience, bearing with one another in love, endeavoring to keep the unity of The Spirit in the bond of Peace.*

*There is one Body and One Spirit, just as you were called in one Hope of your Calling; one Lord, one Faith, one Baptism; one GOD and Father of all, who is above all, and through all, and in you all.*

*But to each one of us, Grace was given according to the measure of Christ's Gift. Therefore He says: "When He ascended on high, He led captivity captive, and gave Gifts to men." And Jesus Himself gave some to be Apostles, some Prophets, some Evangelists, and some Pastors and some Teachers, for the equipping of the Believers for the work of ministry, for the edifying of the Body of Christ, till we all come to the unity of the Faith and of the Knowledge of the Son of GOD, to become a mature person, to the measure of the stature of the fullness of Christ; that we should no longer be children, tossed back and forth and carried about with every wind of doctrine, by the trickery of men, in the cunning craftiness of deceitful plotting, but, speaking the truth in love, may grow up in all things into Him who is the head – the Messiah – from whom the whole Body, joined and knit together by what every joint supplies, according to the effective working by which every part does its share, causes growth of the Body for the edifying of itself in love.*

So, what those Scriptures tell us about Ministries and Offices is this: GOD gives all of Their Children some form of Ministry or Office, although some of us receive more than one of these Ministries or Offices. They are all intended for the Body of Christ, to edify and build the Body, but also to grow the Body by adding more Believers. We are supposed to work together in love, care for one another, and help each other; all Believers, working together. With each Ministry or Office, there will also be Gifts given to Empower us to fulfill our Calling. These are known as "The Gifts of the Holy Spirit".

**The Word of Wisdom** – to give Divine solutions to life's problems. Solomon was a great example of this Gift of Wisdom. People came from all over the world to hear from him because he was so wise. He then wrote Proverbs and Ecclesiastes expressing some of the Wisdom he received from the Holy Spirit. Jesus shows us several examples of this by how He would answer the Scribes, Pharisees, and Sadducees, who were constantly trying to trick Him.

**The Word of Knowledge** – to know something you should not know, but you just know it anyway. This Knowledge will usually just pop into your head, that you know something that you never knew before, and that it will usually help someone in a difficult situation to get closer to GOD. Jesus showed this Gift to us when He knew what others were thinking before they said it out loud. He also knew the whole life of the Samaritan Woman without being told anything about her. Jesus knew that Peter was about to ask Him about Temple Taxes, when they all went to visit the Temple in Capernaum, and He spoke about it before Peter could even say it out loud. Jesus showed this Gift to us when after He healed a blind and mute man, some of the Pharisees committed blasphemy against the Holy Spirit, but Jesus *"knew their thoughts"* as shown in Matthew 12:22-30

**Faith** – as a Gift, is the ability to Believe, despite the evidence, and encourage others to Believe as well. Jesus said, *"If you have Faith the size of a Mustard Seed you could move mountains."* You could speak to something, and it would obey. You could do anything. Faith, that kind of Faith, to truly believe all things are possible with

GOD, and that you apply that Faith to your own actions… is a Gift. This Gift of Faith is different from our faith in GOD and that Jesus died for our sins.


**Gifts of Healings** – is the supernatural ability to Heal the body. Jesus showed us this Healing Gift when He Healed a man with Leprosy. He also gave a Paralyzed man the ability to Walk. Jesus gave sight back to a Blind man by taking some dirt, making some mud, and formed an Eye out of the mud, reminiscent of when GOD made Adam. This type of *Healing through Creation* is something that only GOD can do, or that GOD will empower someone else to do, who was given the Gifts of Healings.


**The Working of Miracles** – is to perform something miraculous that only GOD could do. Jesus showed us this Gift many times; when He turned Water into Wine; when He walked on water; raised a widow's son from the dead; calmed a storm by speaking to it; and fed 5000 people with only 5 loaves of bread and 2 fish. Another time while in Capernaum, Jesus told Peter to go down to the Lake, catch a fish, and within its mouth would be found a Coin to pay the Temple Tax. He also showed this Gift when He had the Disciples cast their Net into the water, and they then hauled up 153 fish.


**Prophecy** – to speak of future events, from Visions, Dreams, or Words directly from the Holy Spirit. Jesus showed us this Gift when He foretold His own death, and also His Resurrection; when He predicted that Judas would betray Him; that Peter would deny Him; that all the Apostles would run, scatter, and hide; He foretold that Believers would be Persecuted after His death; and when He predicted the details of the destruction of the Temple so accurately about 40 years before it happened.

**Discerning of Spirits** – to see into the spirit world, and supernaturally understand and differentiate very detailed information about the Demons and Angels around us. Jesus showed us this Gift when He discerned the 10,000 Demons in a single man of the Gadarenes. He also showed us this Gift when He identified a *"spirit of Infirmity"* in a woman and called it out by name in Luke 13.

**Different Kinds of Tongues** – to speak and understand multiple Languages and Dialects. We are shown this Gift at Pentecost in Acts 2 when the Apostles and Disciples were heard by people of many different Nations praising GOD and speaking about the wonderful things that GOD has done; they not only heard the words in all their own Languages, but also in their own Dialects.

**The Interpretation of Tongues** – to interpret someone who is Speaking in Tongues. I tend to believe this is the highest and least common of the Gifts. I say this because although Paul writes about this Gift in both 1 Corinthians 12 & 14, I can honestly say that I have never seen this Gift exercised in my life as a Christian, nor can I recall ever seeing an example of someone exercising this Gift in the Bible. Paul describes this Gift as being even higher than the Gift of Prophecy, so I feel strongly that it will be seen more and more when the next outpouring of the Holy Spirit occurs… very soon!

In 1 Corinthians, Chapters 12, 13, and 14, Paul writes extensively about the Gifts, so I would suggest you spend some extra time studying these Scriptures below for proper context. One question I have been asked is if all these Gifts apply to both men and women. The answer is Yes, since there are clear examples of this in the Bible. One example of this would be that in both the Old and New Testaments, the word "*Prophetess*" was used many times to describe a female Prophet. I have personally known and received accurate Prophetic Words from several Prophetesses over the years.

*1 Corinthians 12:1 – 14:1-33,39-40*
*Now concerning Spiritual Gifts, brothers and sisters, I do not want you to be ignorant: You know that you were Gentiles, carried away to these dumb Idols however you were led. Therefore, I make known to you that no one speaking by the Spirit of GOD calls Jesus accursed, and no one can say that Jesus is Lord except by the Holy Spirit. There are <u>diversities of Gifts</u>, but the same Spirit. There are <u>differences of Ministries</u>, but the same LORD. And there are diversities of activities, but it is the same GOD who works all in all. But <u>the manifestation of The Spirit is given to each one for the profit of all</u>: for to one is given <u>The Word of Wisdom</u> through The Spirit, to another <u>The Word of Knowledge</u> through the same Spirit, to another <u>Faith</u> by the same Spirit, to another <u>Gifts of Healings</u> by the same Spirit, to another <u>The Working of Miracles</u>, to another <u>Prophecy</u>, to another <u>Discerning of Spirits</u>, to another <u>Different kinds of Tongues</u>, to another <u>The Interpretation of Tongues</u>. But one and the same Spirit works all these things, distributing to each one individually as She Wills.*

*For as the body is one and has many members, but all the members of that one body, being many, are one body, so also is the Messiah.* **For by One Spirit we were all baptized into one Body** – *whether Jews or Greeks, whether slaves or free – and have* **all been made to drink into One Spirit.** *For, in fact, the body is not one member but many. If the foot should say, "Because I am not a hand, I am not of the body," is it therefore not of the body? And if the ear should say, "Because I am not an eye, I am not of the body," is it therefore not of the body? If the whole body were an eye, where would be the hearing? If the whole were hearing, where would be the smelling?* **But now GOD has set the members, each one of them, in the Body just as intended.** *And if they were all one member, where would the Body be? But now indeed there are many members, yet one Body. And the eye cannot say to the hand, "I have no need of you"; nor again the head to the feet, "I have no need of you." But on the contrary, those members of the Body which seem to be weaker are necessary. And those members of the Body which we think to be less honorable, on these we bestow greater honor; and our unpresentable parts have greater modesty, but our presentable parts have no need. But GOD composed the Body, having given greater honor to that part which lacks it, that there should be no division in the Body, but that the members should have the same care for one another. And if one member suffers, all the members suffer with it; or if one member is honored, all the members rejoice with it.*

*Now* **you are the** __Body of Christ__**, and members individually. And GOD has appointed these in the Church: first** __Apostles__**, second** __Prophets__**, third** __Teachers__**, after that** __Miracles__**, then** __Gifts of Healings__**,** __Helps__**,** __Administrations__**,** __varieties of Tongues__**.** *Are all Apostles? Are all Prophets? Are all Teachers? Are all workers of Miracles? Do all have Gifts of Healings? Do all speak with Tongues? Do all interpret?* **But earnestly desire the best Gifts.** *And yet I show you a more excellent way.* **Though I speak with the tongues of men and of Angels,** *but do not have Love, I have become sounding brass or a clanging cymbal. And though I have the Gift of Prophecy, and Understand all Mysteries and all Knowledge, and have a Faith that can move mountains, but do not have Love, I am nothing. And though I bestow all my goods to feed the poor, and though I give my body to be burned, but do not have Love, it profits me nothing.*

*Love suffers long and is kind; Love does not envy; Love does not parade itself, is not arrogant; does not behave rudely, does not seek its own, is not provoked, thinks no evil; does not rejoice in iniquity, but rejoices in the Truth; bears all things, believes all things, hopes all things, endures all things.*

*Love never fails. But whether there are Prophecies, they will fail; whether there are Tongues, they will cease; whether there is Knowledge, it will vanish away. For we Know in part and we Prophesy in part. But when that which is complete has come, then that which is in part will be done away.* (as we become more like Jesus, who was given the Spirit without measure.)

*When I was a child, I spoke as a child, I understood as a child, I thought as a child; but when I became a man, I put away childish things. For now, we see in a mirror, dimly, but then face to face. Now I know in part, but then I shall know just as I also am known. And now Faith, Hope, Love remain, these three; but the greatest of these is Love.*

**Pursue Love, and <u>desire Spiritual Gifts</u>, but especially that you may Prophesy.** *For he who speaks in a Tongue does not speak to men but to GOD, for no one understands him; however, in the Spirit, he speaks Mysteries.* **But he who Prophesies speaks edification and exhortation and comfort to men.** *He who speaks in a Tongue edifies himself, but* **he who Prophesies edifies the Church.** *I wish you all spoke with Tongues, but even more that you*

*Prophesied; for he who Prophesies is greater than he who speaks with Tongues, unless indeed he <u>Interprets</u>, that the Church may receive edification.*

*But now, brothers and sisters, if I come to you speaking with Tongues, what shall I profit you unless I speak to you either by Revelation, by Knowledge, by Prophesying, or by Teaching? Even things without life, whether flute or harp, when they make a sound, unless they make a distinction in the sounds, how will it be known what is piped or played? For if the Trumpet makes an uncertain sound, who will prepare himself for battle? So likewise, you, unless you utter by the tongue words easy to understand, how will it be known what is spoken? For you will be speaking into the air. There are, it may be, so many kinds of Languages in the world, and none of them is without significance. Therefore, if I do not know the meaning of the Language, I shall be a foreigner to him who speaks, and he who speaks will be a foreigner to me. Even so you, **since you are zealous for Spiritual Gifts, let it be for the edification of the Church that you seek to excel.** Therefore, let him who speaks in a Tongue pray that he may Interpret. For if I pray in a Tongue, my spirit prays, but my understanding is unfruitful.*

*What is the conclusion then? I will pray with The Spirit, and I will also pray with the Understanding. I will sing with The Spirit, and I will also sing with the Understanding. Otherwise, if you bless with The Spirit, how will he who occupies the place of the uninformed say "Amen" at your giving of thanks, since he does not understand what you say? For you indeed give thanks well, but the other is not edified. I thank my GOD I speak with Tongues more than you all; yet in the Church, I would rather speak five words with my understanding, that I may teach others also, than ten thousand words in a Tongue. Brothers and sisters, do not be children regarding*

*Understanding; however, in malice be Babes, but in
Understanding be mature.*

*In the Law it is written: "With men of other Tongues and
other lips I will speak to this people; and yet, for all that,
they will not hear Me," says the LORD. Therefore, Tongues
are for a sign, not to those who believe but to Unbelievers;
but Prophesying is not for Unbelievers but for those who
believe. Therefore, if the whole Church comes together in
one place, and all speak with Tongues, and there come in
those who are uninformed or Unbelievers, will they not say
that you are out of your mind?* **But if all <u>Prophesy</u>, and an
Unbeliever or an uninformed person comes in, he is
convinced by all, he is convicted by all. And thus, <u>the
secrets of his heart are revealed; and so, falling down on
his face, he will worship GOD and report that GOD is truly
among you.</u>**

*How is it then, brothers and sisters? Whenever you come
together, each of you has a Psalm, has a Teaching, has a
Tongue, has a Revelation, has an Interpretation. Let all
things be done for edification. If anyone speaks in a
Tongue, let there be two or at the most three, each in turn,
and let one Interpret. But if there is no Interpreter, let him
keep silent in Church, and let him speak to himself and to
GOD. Let two or three Prophets speak, and let the others
judge. But if anything is revealed to another who sits by,
let the first keep silent.* **For <u>you can all Prophesy one by
one, that all may learn, and all may be encouraged</u>.** *And
the spirits of the Prophets are subject to the Prophets.* **<u>For
GOD is not the author of confusion but of Peace, as in all
the Churches of the Believers.</u>**

**<u>Therefore, brothers and sisters, desire earnestly to
Prophesy, and do not forbid to speak with Tongues</u>. Let
all things be done decently and in order.**

## 2 Timothy 1:1-14

*Paul, an Apostle of Jesus, the Messiah, by the Will of GOD, according to the Promise of Life that is in Christ Jesus, to Timothy, a beloved Child:  Grace, Mercy, and Peace from God the Father and Christ Jesus our Lord.*

*I thank GOD, whom I serve, as my ancestors did, with a pure conscience, as I remember you always in my prayers, night and day, greatly desiring to see you, being mindful of your tears, that I may be filled with Joy, when I call to remembrance **the genuine Faith that is in you**, which dwelt first in your grandmother Lois and your mother Eunice, and I am persuaded is in you also.  Therefore, I remind you to **stir up the Gift of GOD which is in you through the laying on of my hands.  For GOD has not given us a spirit of fear, but a Spirit of Power and of Love and of Self-Control.**  So, do not be ashamed of the testimony of our Lord, nor of me His prisoner, but share with me in the sufferings for the Gospel according to the Power of GOD, who has saved us and called us with a holy Calling, not according to our works, but according to His own purpose and Grace which was given to us in Christ Jesus before time began, but has now been revealed by the appearing of our Savior Jesus, the Messiah, who has abolished death and brought Life and immortality to light through the Gospel, to which **I was appointed a Preacher, an Apostle, and a Teacher.**  For this reason, I also suffer these things, yet I am not ashamed, for I know whom I have believed and am persuaded that I am able to guard the deposit that has been entrusted to me until that Day. Embrace and follow the pattern of sound words which you have heard from me, in Faith and Love, which are in Christ Jesus.  **Guard that good deposit, which was entrusted to you by the Holy Spirit, the One who dwells in us.***

*Therefore **we must pay much closer attention to what we have heard, lest we drift away from it.*** *For since the message declared by Angels proved to be reliable, and every transgression or disobedience received a just retribution, how shall we Escape if we neglect such a great salvation?* ***It was declared at first by the Lord, and it was attested to us by those who heard, while GOD also bore witness*** *(Confirmed)* ***by Signs and Wonders and various Miracles and <u>by the Gifts distributed from the Holy Spirit</u>, according to GOD's Will.***

Don't make the mistake of believing those who claim that Gifts and the Power of the Holy Spirit don't exist any longer today. Paul even warned Timothy about this disbelief happening in the future. The future that is currently upon us now.

*But know this, that **in the Last Days**, perilous times will come: For men will be lovers of themselves, lovers of money, boasters, proud, blasphemers, disobedient to parents, unthankful, unholy, unloving, unforgiving, slanderers, without self-control, brutal, despisers of good, traitors, headstrong, arrogant, lovers of pleasure rather than lovers of GOD, **having a form of godliness <u>but denying GOD's Power</u>**. And from such people turn away!*

So many "Christians" I know, and so many Churches, do not teach about having an ongoing relationship and dialogue with the Holy Spirit, Walking in the Gifts and Power of the Holy Spirit, or the Art of Spiritual Warfare. Not only do they no longer teach it, but some teach that it doesn't even exist anymore. It truly amazes me that people so readily go along with this teaching, even though Jesus Himself practiced and taught His Apostles and Disciples to exercise these Gifts and principles. Paul, who wrote the majority of the New Testament, not only practiced these Gifts and principles, but also taught extensively about it, by devoting whole Chapters and even entire Books to the teaching of these topics.

Those who do not have a genuine Faith, and do not believe in the Power and Giftings of the Holy Spirit, will not experience these Blessings and Giftings from the Holy Spirit due to their unbelief. Then, because they don't experience anything, rather than Repenting so they can experience Her Power, they teach others that these Gifts are no longer available to ALL Believers. This way they can feel better about not having a personal relationship, nor any Gifts, by lying to themselves and others that it no longer exists. So, this way they can still feel good about themselves, convinced they did nothing wrong that would have caused them to miss out. So very unwise!

Ultimately, the Scriptures plainly show us that these Gifts are meant to help us navigate through this life, and help us to continue to Walk forward. They are used to prove that GOD is alive and well, and within us. If these Gifts are not active in your life, or in your Church, you need to ask yourself, "_Why?_". Some people say that they are no longer active, but these people are just making excuses to you for why "They" are not given these Gifts. Quite honestly, ask yourself why would the Holy Spirit give such wonderful Gifts to rebellious and ungrateful children, even if they were a Child of GOD? Would you, if it was your child who was being disobedient and ungrateful?

I have seen these Gifts active in myself, and in many, many others. I have also never read anywhere in the Bible that states that even though the Scriptures had Prophesied about the Gifts to come, and New Testament writers wrote so extensively about them, that they have somehow stopped. This makes no sense, especially since the purpose of GOD giving us these Gifts has not changed after all these many years. The purpose of the Great Commission was to go out into the world and share, not only the Gospel of Jesus, but also to prove that GOD is still very much alive and well.

You need to ask yourself this question, and answer honestly, "Has the need for the whole world to hear about Jesus, and be shown evidence of GOD's Love really gone away?" If your honest answer is, "No!", then you need to seek after these Gifts diligently, so you will be able to impact your world for the Kingdom of GOD, and fulfill your Calling. Jesus made it abundantly clear that the "Gifts of the Holy Spirit" and "The Great Commission" go hand in hand, and that He hasn't changed.

*Acts 1:4-5,8*
*On one occasion, while Jesus was with them, He gave them this Command: "Do not leave Jerusalem, but **wait for the Promise of the Father; that which you have heard Me say, 'For John truly baptized with water, but you will be baptized with the Holy Spirit.'** not many days from now. But **you shall receive Power when the Holy Spirit has come upon you; and you shall be witnesses to Me in Jerusalem, and in all Judea and Samaria, and to the end of the Earth.**"*

*Hebrews 13:8-9*
*Jesus Christ is the **same** yesterday, today, and forever. **Do not be led away by various and strange doctrines.***

The following Scriptures give us examples of Natural and Spiritual Gifts, and how they manifested in the lives of Believers.


*Exodus 31:1-5*
*Then **the LORD said** to Moses, "See, I have chosen Bezalel, and **I have filled him with the Spirit of GOD**, in Wisdom, in Understanding, in Knowledge, and in all manner of Workmanship**, to design artistic works, to work in gold, in silver, in bronze, in cutting jewels for setting stones, in carving wood, and to engage in all manner of workmanship."*


That is a perfect example of GOD-given Talents, where GOD had Supernaturally provided Talents to a man in the Natural.


*1 Peter 1:10-12*
*Concerning this salvation, **the Prophets have inquired and searched carefully, who Prophesied of the Grace that would come to you, searching what, or what manner of time, the Spirit of the Messiah who was in them, testifying beforehand regarding the sufferings of the Messiah, and the glories that would follow. To them, it was revealed that, not to themselves, but to you, they were ministering the things which now have been reported to you through those who have preached the Gospel to you, by the Holy Spirit sent from Heaven**, the things which even Angels desire to look into.*

*Mark 12:36*
Jesus speaking: *"For **King David himself <u>said by the Holy Spirit</u>:** 'The L<small>ORD</small> said to my Lord, "Sit at My right-hand, till I make Your enemies Your footstool." ' "*


*Acts 1:15-16*
*In those days, Peter stood up among the Believers – a group numbering about a hundred and twenty – and said, "Brothers and sisters, **the Scripture had to be fulfilled in which <u>the Holy Spirit spoke long ago through David</u>** concerning Judas, who served as a guide for those who arrested Jesus."*


*Acts 28:25-28*
*The people disagreed among themselves and began to leave after Paul had made this final statement: **"Rightly <u>the Holy Spirit spoke by the Prophet Isaiah</u>** to your ancestors, saying...*


The point of showing those Scriptures is to simply answer the question of whether or not the Holy Spirit worked through those written about in the Old Testament. The Holy Spirit was around and had Gifted certain individuals, usually Kings and Prophets, specific people who had particular Callings back then. In this case, David was a King and wrote Prophetic songs, which is what the Psalms are... they are the Lyrics to songs that David wrote through the inspiration of the Holy Spirit.

*Acts 11:28*
*One of them, named Agabus, stood up and **through the Power of the Holy Spirit predicted that a severe famine would spread** over the entire Roman world, **which actually occurred** during the reign of Claudius Caesar.*


*Luke 1:67*
*And Zacharias, John's father, **was filled with the Holy Spirit, and Prophesied about the future**:*


Those above were two of the many Scriptures that are examples of how the Holy Spirit operates in us regarding the Gift of Prophecy to help the Body of Christ. There are many other examples of ordinary people throughout the Bible that are shown operating in their Gifts. This is one example that Luke wrote about below.


*Luke 2:25-28*
*And behold, there was a man in Jerusalem whose name was Simeon, and this man was just and devout, waiting for the Consolation of Israel, and **the Holy Spirit was upon him**. And **it had been revealed to him by the Holy Spirit** that he would not see death before he had seen the LORD's Messiah. So, he came **by The Spirit** into the Temple. And when the parents brought in the Infant Jesus, to do for Him according to the custom of the Law, he took Him up in his arms and **blessed GOD** and **spoke a Prophecy** over Jesus.*

## Is The Holy Spirit In Us Or On Us?

Well, the answer is usually, Both! In general, there has been some confusion with many Believers I have come across about the Holy Spirit coming ***into us*** when we are Born-Again, compared to the Power that will come ***upon us*** to activate our Gifts and Empower us to perform the Office that we were called to.

Here are a few of examples clarifying this difference. In John 20, after Jesus' Resurrection, but before He went back to Heaven, Jesus does something interesting, He personally provides the Apostles with the Holy Spirit for their Re-Birth. John wrote this,

*John 20:21-22*
*So, **Jesus said to them** again, "Peace to you! As the Father has sent Me, I also send you." And when He had said this, **He breathed on them**, and said to them, "Receive the Holy Spirit."*

What is interesting is that almost immediately after this event, Jesus tells the Apostles to stay in Jerusalem until the Holy Spirit is poured out ***upon*** them to receive Power. This statement was shown to us in Acts 1 when Luke wrote this:

*Acts 1:4-5,8*
*On one occasion, while Jesus was with them, **He gave them this Command: "Do not leave Jerusalem, but wait for the Promise of the Father; that which you have heard Me say, 'For John truly baptized with water, but you will be baptized with the Holy Spirit.' not many days from now. But you shall <u>receive Power</u> when the Holy Spirit has come <u>upon you</u>, and you shall be witnesses to Me in Jerusalem... and to the end of the Earth."***

Interestingly, there was actually a situation where Paul found "Believers" that had not received the Power of the Holy Spirit ***upon*** them yet, because they had not even heard of the Holy Spirit. So, Paul then "Laid Hands" on them and changed that. We see that Luke wrote about this in Acts 19 saying:

*Acts 19:1-2,6*
*And it happened, while Apollos was at Corinth, that **Paul**, having passed through the upper regions, came to Ephesus. And **finding some Disciples** there, he said to them, "**Did you receive the Holy Spirit <u>when you Believed</u>?**" So, they said to him, "**We have not so much as heard whether there is a Holy Spirit.**" And **when Paul had Laid Hands on them, the Holy Spirit came <u>upon them</u>, and they spoke with Tongues and Prophesied.** Now the men were about twelve in all.*

This Scripture is a good example that shows us clearly that there is a distinct difference between the Holy Spirit coming ***into us*** as Believers when we first believe and are Born-Again, and when the Holy Spirit comes ***upon us*** to Empower us in our Gifts, which was then revealed by them Speaking in Tongues and Prophesying.

There are many other Scriptures convey these ideas, but in Summary, I think I would express it this way:

**Re-Birth:** When we are Born-Again, the Holy Spirit fills the "Empty Place" within us, designed for the Holy Spirit to fill, since we are the "*Temple of the Holy Spirit*". Once we accept Jesus as our Lord and Savior, the Holy Spirit will come ***into us***, so that person can no longer be filled (Possessed) with a Demon, like with an "Unbeliever". This event is like a "switch", where we are either an Unbeliever and would go to hell, or a Believer and will go to Heaven. There is no process… you are either a Believer or an Unbeliever… there is no in-between state. The Holy Spirit is either within you, or not within you. Here are some basic examples of this:

*Ezekiel 36:26-28*
The LORD GOD speaking: ***"I will give you a new Heart and put a new spirit within you; and I will remove the Heart of stone from your Flesh, and give you a Heart of flesh and blood. I will put My Spirit <u>within you</u> and cause you to walk in My Decrees, and you will be careful to observe My Ordinances… so you will be My people, and I will be your God."***

*John 14:17*
***"She*** (Holy Spirit) ***resides with you, and will be <u>in you</u>.***"

**Power:** When we are Empowered by the Holy Spirit coming ***<u>upon us</u>***, we are given the Power to operate in our Giftings and Office. This Power can come all at once, as it did with Jesus, or, what happens most often, is that a *measure* of Power comes initially, then increases at different times when we get promoted to new levels. This Power flows in us, and through us to others. Jesus described it this way when He said in John7:38-39, *"Whoever Believes in Me, as Scripture has said: 'Out of their hearts will flow rivers of <u>Living Water</u>.' "* *Jesus was talking about the Holy Spirit.*" The Greek word "*heart*" used here is that "Empty Place" that was Filled.

I would like to provide you with some practical advice on how to operate in your Office and your Gifts.  These are Gems of Wisdom that I have collected over the years that will help you navigate through them.

I can't stress this to you enough… Do not take on an Office or Role unless you are told directly from the Holy Spirit, and it is Confirmed with others.  This also applies to the performing of Gifts that the Holy Spirit did _not_ give you.  You will fail, and you will take others down with you.  _I have seen this happen!_

One way to encourage our receiving more Revelation from the Holy Spirit is this:  Write down or record what you hear or see in your Visions, Dreams, or Words given to you; this will show respect to the Holy Spirit for actually speaking to you.  I would also suggest putting a Journal or Tape Recorder next to your bed for Dreams, and carry them with you for Visions and Words, so they are readily available.  This will also help to remind you later when these things come true, which will strengthen your faith as well as others.

Pay attention to the Character of the Voices you hear within you.  You can hear from the Holy Spirit, the Father, Jesus, Angels, Demons, or from your own Flesh, and you need to be able to differentiate between all of them, and to Test them.  Here are a couple of examples of this:

*Matthew 10:19-20*

Jesus speaking: *"But when they arrest you, **do not worry about what to say or how to say it. At that time, you will be given what to say, for it will not be you speaking, but the <u>Spirit of your Father speaking through you</u>.***"

*Mark 13:9-11*

Jesus speaking: *"But watch out for yourselves, for they will betray you and deliver you to Tribunals and to Churches. You will be beaten and brought before rulers and kings for My sake, and for a testimony to them. And the Gospel must first be preached to all the Nations. But when they arrest you and deliver you up, **do not worry beforehand about what you will speak. But whatever is given you in that hour, speak that, <u>for it is not you who speaks, but the Holy Spirit</u>.***"

     Jesus gave us many examples of the Gifts He operated with, for example: How he just "Knew" what people's thoughts were; how He answered "Wisely"; how He Healed people; how He cast out Demons; and how He would Shepherd the people. I can tell you from my own personal experience that many times while talking with someone, or counseling them, and in the Natural, I have no idea what to say to help them. They tell me how their life is crumbling, and all these bad things are happening, and within myself, I am thinking, "I really have no clue what to say to them!" So, while I am listening to them, I am also praying that the Holy Spirit would give me a Word of Wisdom or a Word of Knowledge, so I can help them. And all of a sudden, out of nowhere, something comes to me, so I speak it to them, and their life changes. Just like the lights went on in a dark room, and they say, "That's it!". But, it is clearly not me, and it wouldn't be you either; it is the Holy Spirit giving us the Wisdom to Know what to say, so all the credit and glory goes to GOD. We are given a Word of Knowledge or Word of Wisdom to help them with life, or to answer the questions that are really hard to know what to say at times. We all go through crazy times in life, and the idea that we are able to get an answer from GOD directly is incredible, but is readily available to all of us, as one of Their Children, if we would only ask.

For those of you who do get Words from the Holy Spirit, and I know many of you have… this warning applies to you. If you receive a positive or a negative Word for yourself, or for others, but you have an _emotional tie_ to the topic, then _don't trust it_; get Confirmation from multiple sources before you act. Your Flesh may be involved in that Word, and if it is, you will end up going the wrong direction. Full disclosure, this has happened to me before, and others I know, and I can tell you from experience, the results can be very painful. So, if you get a Word about yourself, you need to bring things into the light, don't keep it to yourself, so the darkness has no control or influence over you, or over the Word.

For example, if you feel you were told that a specific person is "The One" that GOD is giving you, seek Counsel from others who hear from the Holy Spirit, so you can get Confirmation if it's true, or Guidance if it is not true. But again, do not get counsel from someone with an emotional tie to the answer, because then their Flesh might get involved, in the same way, your Flesh could be involved in the emotional topic. This goes for men and women alike, that when we are trying to operate in the Spirit, we need to make sure we act on the Words we receive, but if we have an emotional tie to it, we must get Confirmation, and bring it into the light.

In general, do not make any important decisions without Confirmation; the bigger the decision, the more Confirmation you should get.  I have known several people who have actually decided they *think* something is best, so they make the decision and do it, but then after it starts going very wrong, they will then think… "You know, I should probably pray about this to get an answer!"  But they had already done it.  So, my advice… is Pray First!  And this is really important… *silence is not a Yes*!  Silence means you are to wait on the LORD for an answer or guidance.  You will eventually get an answer, so don't just ask, and when you don't get an answer right away, act on the silence as if it were a Yes answer.

If you get a Word about someone else, never share that Word with others, unless you are released to share it by the Holy Spirit, or by the person the Word is about.  Because, Gossiping is a Sin, as is mentioned a great deal in both the Old and New Testaments, so you risk losing your Gifts and Office.

How do you know "The Truth" when you hear it?  If someone speaks to you about something spiritual, or you hear a voice inside you; goosebumps and chills are one way, but when it is from the Holy Spirit, it is known as "Confirmation", although some Bibles use the phrase "*Bear Witness*", and it usually comes with a "*Peace that surpasses all understanding.*"  As you develop and grow in your relationship with the Holy Spirit, you will come to better understand the character of the voices you are hearing, and the character of the experience, so you will know absolutely without a doubt or a reservation, that you are hearing Truth, and that you are receiving that Confirmation from the Holy Spirit.

Some of you may have felt chills, goosebumps, or your hair standing on end when you were around something evil, so how can we tell the difference between good and evil chills or goosebumps?  Well, very early on in my Christian Walk, I would sometimes get chills or goosebumps, and at first, I could not immediately tell the difference. Later, as I developed a closer relationship with GOD, I began to quickly Discern the difference. I would describe it this way, that when you feel a spiritual presence, good or evil, you get a physical expression on your body like chills, goosebumps, or hair standing on end, but more importantly, it is accompanied by additional indicators. If it is evil, then you may feel a "cringe" or "shiver", similar to someone scratching a chalkboard, or a deep sense of fear, despair, rage, anger, depression, or anxiety; but that would be dependent on the type of Demon it was. If it is the Father, Jesus, the Holy Spirit, or an Angel, then you will feel a deep sense of Peace, Love, Warmth, or Joy, along with your chills or goosebumps. This also, like the "Confirmation" I mentioned earlier, is an indicator of Truth. Both of those processes of Discernment will grow and become easier to distinguish between good and evil as you begin to understand the "character of good" compared to the "character of evil".

In 1 Corinthians 13:9, Paul writes, *"For we Know in part and we Prophesy in part"*. Now, as we have also seen in many other Scriptures, this means that we are all given Power and our Giftings *"in measure"*. None of us are given every piece of the puzzle. So, we don't Know everything, or Prophesy everything about a situation, so as time goes on, we get more details, or the other pieces of the puzzle will come from someone else, which will then allow you to see the puzzle picture more clearly. Understanding this concept is very important, because you need to know that you will not get all the details, and you will have to operate in Faith and wait on the LORD to grow and deepen your Faith. You are not going to know everything, you are not going to get everything, you are not going to figure it all out, and you may need to get part of it from someone else. You may get some directly, or you may get some indirectly, through your Spouse, your friends, your family, a co-worker, or even a complete stranger. So, you never know where the details are going to come from, because you do not know everything, and must rely on others in the Body to see GOD's plans for us or others. This principle is particularly important, so we won't have a false expectation that we will know everything. When I am in this type of situation, I like to just say... "We'll just keep Walking it out."

If you abuse or neglect your Gifts, you will lose them. For example, as I briefly touched on earlier, you share details with others that a person told you in confidence, or specific details said to you in confidence directly from the Holy Spirit. I have been told very personal details about people's lives directly from the Holy Spirit, but, it was not for me to share with others, it was either for a discussion I was having with that person, or just for me to better understand what that person was going through so I could more accurately pray for them, but it was definitely not for me to share with others.

Another example of this abuse is if someone has taken money to share their Gift. I have known of people that have done this, and the result was that they quickly lost their Gifts. One was a Prophet who decided to start charging money to give out Prophetic Words. At first, he made a lot of money, but then he lost all his Gifts and fell hard. People can choose to abuse their Gifts since we have Free Will, but there will be consequences for doing that. Remember the Parable of the Talents? The servant that was given only one Talent but had neglected and abused his Gift by burying it. So, instead of using the one Talent he was given from the Lord, he chose not to so he was rebuked when his Lord returned, and was then kicked out. We all have Free Will, so we can choose to take GOD-given Gifts and ruin them. Therefore, it is essential that we do not neglect them, or abuse them, or use them for anything other than what GOD has intended.

## Luke 11:1-13

*Now it came to pass, as Jesus was praying in a certain place, when He ceased, that one of His Disciples said to Him, "Lord, teach us to pray, as John the Baptist also taught his Disciples."*

*So, Jesus said to them, "When you pray, say:*

*'Our Father in Heaven, Holy is Your Name. Your Kingdom come. Your Will be done, as it is in Heaven, so let it be done on Earth. Give us each day our daily bread. And forgive us our sins, for we also forgive everyone who has sinned against us. And do not lead us into Testing, but deliver us from the Evil One.' "*

*And then He said to them, "Which of you shall have a friend, and go to him at midnight and say to him, 'Friend, lend me three loaves; for a friend of mine has come to me on his journey, and I have nothing to set before him'; and he will answer from within and say, 'Do not trouble me; the door is now shut, and my children are with me in bed; I cannot rise and give to you'? I say to you, though he will not rise and give to him because he is his friend, yet because of his persistence, he will rise and give him as many as he needs. So, **I say to you, ask, and keep asking, and it will be given to you; seek, and keep seeking, and you will find; knock, and keep knocking, and it will be opened to you. For everyone who asks receives, and he who seeks finds, and to him who knocks it will be opened.** If a son asks for bread from any father among you, will he give him a stone? Or if he asks for a fish, will he give him a snake instead of a fish? Or if he asks for an egg, will he offer him a scorpion?*

***If you then, being evil, know how to give good Gifts to your children, <u>how much more will the Heavenly Father give the Holy Spirit to those who ask Him!</u>"***

Luke 11 tells us plainly that if we desire to have more Gifts, we simply need to ask the Father, through our relationship with the Holy Spirit, and more will be given. If you want more of your current Gifts, or new Gifts, then you need to develop your relationship with the Holy Spirit. By having a dialogue about this, you will come to a better understanding of your Calling, the Gifts you have been given, and the Gifts you will be provided. You will have a passion within you for your Calling and Gifts within the deepest part of who you are, and a desire to help people within the scope of those Gifts and Calling. So, have that conversation with the Holy Spirit and ask for Words, Dreams, and Visions, or for others to speak a Word to you, so you will better understand who you are, and you *will* see it happen. I cannot tell you how times I have told people to do this exact thing, for them to ask the Holy Spirit, so they do, and it happens. It is nothing that I am doing, I am just pointing them to the One who they need to be in a deeper relationship with, in order for them to fulfill their Calling in the LORD.

One thing I see that is profoundly lacking in most Churches today, is the support for the Body to practice their Gifts. We need to encourage people to practice their Giftings in a safe environment, free of judgement, or ridicule. There is so much more that can be done in Church, in small groups, in-home Churches, or in Bible Studies, especially from Leadership, to open up the discussion for people to share their experiences. We need to encourage them to speak and share if they get a Word, or a Sentence, or a Vision, or a Dream, or a Prophecy, or feel that prayer for Healing or Deliverance is needed, or to share words of encouragement or a Testimony about what GOD is doing. The people genuinely need to feel comfortable sharing their experiences, in an orderly manner of course, that all may learn and grow in their faith.

They need to be given the opportunity to say, "I got a Word, but I don't know if it applies to you." and know that no one will judge them, or even worse, ridicule them. Each person can take turns sharing, one by one, to exercise their Gift, and see what happens. When you give an opportunity for the Holy Spirit to move, and invite Her into your gathering, then She _will_ show up and move mightily in the Body of Believers, and speak to you in ways you would never have expected. Myself, I personally feel more comfortable showing up where I am welcomed, so be sure to invite Her. All these things strengthen and build up the Faith of the Body, and must not only be allowed, but should be encouraged in order for others to be able to grow. Paul wrote about this to the Corinthians.

### _1 Corinthians 14_

_For you can all Prophesy one by one, that all may learn, and all may be encouraged. And the spirits of the Prophets are subject to the Prophets. For GOD is not the author of confusion but of Peace, as in all the Churches of the Believers._

_Therefore, brothers and sisters, desire earnestly to Prophesy, and do not forbid to speak with Tongues. Let all things be done decently and in order._

GOD is looking to do something new and unique. So, all the things that you have already heard or read about, may not be the way the Holy Spirit will manifest in you, providing you are truly open to it, and give a place for Her to operate. I never expected to receive the Revelation I did about who the Holy Spirit truly is; even after I received it, that idea still seemed extraordinary to me, but GOD did it, the Holy Spirit spoke to me, and I received the Revelation. Each of us needs to develop our own relationship so we can become whatever new thing that GOD is looking to do in us, and with us.

During the time of Pentecost, when the Holy Spirit was first poured out, people did all these strange new things that had never been done before. But back then, none of it had happened before, and they were walking down a path that had never been walked before. Jesus said that we would do "*greater things*", and when the new outpouring comes, we will all go to mighty new levels in our Gifts.

I want you to think about this: Imagine when the Holy Spirit gets poured out on us, that one of you receives The Gift of Healings, and you could just go up to someone who has lost arms, legs, or any other body part, and you lay hands on them, and it comes back! That is crazy! Right? Well, that is precisely where we are going! Again, imagine you have the Gift of Different Kinds of Languages, and you go to many other countries to Minister, and you will be able to speak all of their native Languages and Dialects. Is that really possible? Absolutely! It says it in the Bible that it will happen, so why wouldn't GOD do it? We are coming to a time of the Final Revival before The End, when GOD is going to go to a powerful new level, where GOD's Power is going to be poured out on the Body in a way that no one is expecting, or could even imagine. This is coming, regardless of whether you believe it or not! Do you want to be part of it?

All of those Gifts will be raised to an extreme level, but as it says in the "Parable of the Ten Virgins", if you don't have the Oil (*a relationship with the Holy Spirit*) it will not be happening for you! Now, me personally, I want to be part of the Holy Spirit's new "Wave of Fire" that will spread across this world. I want to be one of those people who Heals people in that radical way. I want to be someone who could walk up to an area of Forest that had been burned, and Lay Hands on the ground, and the trees would instantly come back. Is all this really possible?  Yes!  We will do "*greater things*" than Jesus did while He was here, when the Holy Spirit will be poured out this final time.  People do, and have done, truly miraculous things in the name of Jesus, and by the Power of the Holy Spirit, but we are going to a new and different place.  So, the question is, since we all have Free-Will, you need to ask yourself this… "Do I want to be a part of this final move of the Holy Spirit?"  Because if the answer is "Yes!", and you genuinely do want to be included to make a huge difference in your community, and the world, then you must develop a deeper relationship with the Holy Spirit, and know who you are, know your Calling, and know your Gifts.  And if you have questions, talk to someone who you know that is hearing clearly from the Holy Spirit, someone who can help you deepen your relationship.  Ultimately, by your developing that more in-depth relationship with the Holy Spirit; that is where you will get all your questions answered… "*She will teach you all things*", as Jesus said plainly in John 14.

As we mature in our Office and in our Gifts, we get promoted, just like the Military Hierarchy I mentioned before.  As it says in the Scriptures, when we grow in our Gifts, GOD sees that we have been faithful with a little, so GOD will give us more.  As GOD sees that They can trust you with your Gifts, with whatever you are given, then you are given more, you go higher, and are given a Promotion.  I can tell you from my own experiences over the years, that I have gone through several Promotions and Levels.  For example, when I first started doing Spiritual Warfare, it was a real effort; there were times when some attack would come, and I would pray for hours straight, struggling, getting beat up spiritually, and having a very hard time to achieve victory.  But as the years have gone by, and I have been promoted many times, because I was faithful with what I was given, I then became stronger.  With these promotions, I've received new spiritual weapons, like a larger Flaming Sword, or stronger Armor, or you could get a Bow & Arrows, that during your warfare, you are now able to use. Now, personally, I have seen in the Spirit, explosions of a Wall of Fire, like an Atomic Bomb that goes off when I am praying that just wipes them all out. This has actually happened to Rowena and I both while praying over a major City, that this explosion occurred over the whole City. This is very different from where I started, and as I have gone through these different levels, the LORD has said, "I want to elevate you and bring you higher." or "I want to promote you and give you something." so there is something that was received; it is tangible, and you feel it, because you are actually given something very real in the Spirit. And once it happens, you grow and feel stronger; all of a sudden in the Spirit, as you are fighting something evil, it has become easier. So now, I can just speak a Word, a very short phrase, I speak in Tongues, and Boom, there is an explosion in the Spirit, and it is done... they are gone, destroyed.

This is very, very different from where I first started, because my strength and abilities in the Spirit have grown. It is the same with all the Gifts. You use them, you exercise them, you respect them, you show your appreciation for what you are given, you keep track of what you are shown, and you do what you are supposed to do. And, as you do all that, you will get promoted and grow, and you will see and feel the difference. Your Faith will grow to the point that you just believe and know that all things are truly possible. You will know this in the depths of your Soul, that it is not just a catchy phrase that "religious people" say when they claim, "All things are possible!" but they truly don't believe it. It is not like that! You just Know and Believe that you can do some truly amazing things in the Spirit, like after Pentecost, and you know that you are going to. Why? Because you have been told and shown that you will. And you believe it, and know it, deep within your spirit and Soul. That is the Gift of Faith! You genuinely believe, despite how crazy it sounds. Different Gifts manifest differently, but you need to exercise them, and you will be promoted and grow.

An example that you can read about, or listen to for yourself, is regarding a man who was in Ministry for nearly 60 years, and operated at an extremely high level in the Gift of Faith. His name was Henry Gruver, but unfortunately, he recently passed away in October of 2019 at the age of 77. If you want to see someone who truly operated in this Gift of Faith, then study his life, because that man had Faith, and truly Believed! He would go to many places around the world, and then Walk & Pray over the land that he was told to go to, and he would break curses, tear down strongholds, and would see changes occur in the Natural. Many things that he did throughout his life were simply amazing! One amazing example I can remember most of the details surrounding it, was when he was told by the Holy Spirit to go to Taiwan in 2015 and walk around a specific place and pray. But, this area had an active plague going on that was caused by a Mosquito infestation and was afflicting many that would get sick and die very painful deaths within only a few days. The people around him thought he had lost his mind and were fearful for him, but he had Faith that he had Dominion and would be fine, so he went anyway. While walking the area, he had a Vision of a Dragonfly. Immediately after, as he was actually in prayer with a group of people, a large swarm of Dragonflies came overhead and were eating all the Mosquitoes in the area, since that is one of their foods, so the plague ended in the land. All the people were amazed that GOD used his Faith and his Belief to manifest something so real in the Natural to help the people.

You can actually watch a video about "The Dragonfly Miracle" and others on YouTube:  https://youtu.be/kgthUL2xl6I

He also showed us more examples of his Faith when he raised his Wife and kids from the dead, Healed them, and many others.

But, the point to all this is that our Gifts will grow and get stronger, as we Walk them out, continue to Believe, read the Word, get deeper in the Word, allow the Word to get into us, develop a closer relationship with the Holy Spirit, and our Calling and Gifts will become more evident in our lives.

So, really, what does all this have to do with you right now? Well, when we read about the Faithful Believers compared to the Unfaithful Believers, we see a sharp contrast. And, No I am not talking about Unbelievers, I am talking about Believers. Jesus once asked a profound question… *"Who do you say I am?"* And those who claimed to be Believers, but did not show any Fruit of the Spirit, what did Jesus say? *"I never knew you!"*

Our relationship is Key! It is why we were created in the first place; that is, to fellowship with GOD Almighty. So, how can we do that? It is through our relationship with the Holy Spirit. But, we cannot have a "Fruitful" relationship with someone that we don't even understand who that Person is that we are speaking with.

The "Parable of the Ten Virgins" is a good example of this. There were ten Virgins (Believers), and when the Bridegroom (Jesus) came back to *"Gather"* the Bride (the Church Body) to the Marriage Feast, but only five of them were taken; the *"Wise Virgins"* who were prepared with Oil. And what is the Oil symbolic for that allows for Fire and Light? It is the Holy Spirit!!!

Jesus stated this in Matthew 25, referring to the "End Times" or "Last Days", which is, in fact, *our current time*:

*Matthew 25:1-13*

*"Then the Kingdom of Heaven shall be likened to Ten
Virgins who took their lamps and went out to meet the
Bridegroom.* ***Now five of them were Wise, and five were
Foolish****. Those who were Foolish took their lamps and
took no Oil with them, but* **the Wise took Oil** *in their vessels
with their lamps. But while the Bridegroom was delayed in
His return, they all slumbered and slept. And at midnight,
a cry was heard: 'Behold, the Bridegroom is coming; go
out to meet Him!' Then all those Virgins arose and
trimmed their lamps. And the Foolish said to the Wise,
'Give us some of your Oil, for our lamps are going out.'
But the Wise answered, saying, 'No, there may not be
enough for both us and you; but go rather to those who
sell, and buy some for yourselves.' And while they went to
buy,* **the Bridegroom came, and those who were ready
went in with Him to the Wedding, and the door was shut***.
Afterward, the other Virgins came also, saying, 'Lord,
Lord, open to us!' But* **He answered and said, 'Assuredly,
I say to you, I do not know you.' Watch therefore, for you
know neither the Day nor the Hour in which the Son of
Man is coming back.***"

The "Parable of the Ten Virgins" (*above*) was given by Jesus in Matthew 25:1-13. This conversation took place two days before the Passover meal, which has been referred to as "The Last Supper". This Parable, along with other Parables and Teachings, was given by Jesus in response to the "Three Questions" (*below*) that the Disciples asked Him in Matthew 24, where it states:

*Matthew 24:3*

*"Now as Jesus sat on the Mount of Olives, the Disciples
came to Him privately, saying,* **"Tell us,** <u>**when will these
things be**</u>**? And what will be the** <u>**sign of Your coming**</u>**, and
the** <u>**sign of the end of the age**</u>**?"***

Jesus then gives us very long answers to these three questions. All of Matthew 24 and Matthew 25 are focused on these answers. These two Chapters discuss the Tribulation Periods, His Gathering of us to Him (Rapture), and His Second Coming. Both of these Chapters clearly focus on the End Times.

The "Parable of the Two Servants", (in Matthew 24:45-51) came right before the "Parable of the Ten Virgins", and shows us a contrast between the Faithful and the Unfaithful Servants (Believers).

The "Parable of the Ten Virgins" (in Matthew 25:1-13) shows us a contrast between the Wise Virgins (Faithful Believers) who have a close relationship with the Holy Spirit (*Wisdom*), have been filled with Oil and Empowered by Her, and who will be Gathered during the Rapture, compared to the Foolish Virgins (Unfaithful Believers) who will be Left Behind, along with the Unbelievers.

A clear indication of the context of the "Parable of the Ten Virgins" comes at the end of the Parable in Matthew 25 where Jesus says:

*Matthew 25:13*
*"Watch therefore, for you know neither the Day nor the Hour in which the **Son of Man is coming back**."*

The Parable following the "Parable of the Ten Virgins" was the "Parable of the Talents" (in Matthew 25:14-30, on page 171) and was about Believers using our Talents (Skills, Gifts, Office) properly for GOD, or Believers misusing them, without consideration for others, or for why GOD gave us the Talents in the first place.

Notice that all three Parables were addressed to "Believers". There is a similar statement by Jesus in Revelation 3, also addressed to the Believers in the "*Lukewarm*" Church, where He said,

*Revelation 3:15-17*
*"I know your works, that you are neither cold* (Unbeliever) *nor hot* (Faithful Believer). *I could wish you were cold or hot. So then, because you are Lukewarm,* (an Unfaithful Believer) *and neither cold nor hot, I will vomit you out of My mouth. Because you say, 'I am rich, have become wealthy, and have need of nothing' – and do not know that you are wretched, miserable, poor, blind, and naked..."*

Think about that for a moment...

The good news is that the Holy Spirit is reaching out to all of you right now. She is looking to raise you up to a new level of relationship with Them, as Their children, through Her Power, and Giftings. She is looking to make you into Wise, Fruitful Children, and Faithful Believers.

# CHAPTER SEVENTEEN

# WALKING IN THE SPIRIT

To "*Walk in the Spirit*" means that we Walk through our lives with reliance on, fellowship with, and in relationship with the Holy Spirit. We acknowledge that once we are Born-Again, that She resides in us and that She will: Speak with us, Teach us, Guide us, Lead us, Direct our Steps, Confirm Truth, Enable us, Warn us, Protect us, Help us to Pray & Worship, Help us to know the Will of the Father, Point us to Her Son Jesus, Empower us to Fight, Speak through us, and Use us to Minister to others.

One thing I have come to realize is just how sensitive the Holy Spirit is. Similar to our earthly mothers, She can get Her feelings hurt. She is Jealous to spend time with us, have a relationship with us, and speak with us. She grieves when Her Children are hurting, and gets Angry when Her Children are abused or killed. We are told that we can Grieve Her by our actions, since She is being forced to participate in our sins, because She dwells within us (*we are the Temple of the Holy Spirit*). Try to keep that in mind next time you decide to sin intentionally as a Believer, since we are dragging Her into that sin with us. We also have seen how protective Jesus was of Her. The more you learn about Her, the easier it is to understand why He would feel that way about His Mother. We are also warned not to "*Quench*" the Holy Spirit, meaning not to put out the Fire, or to stop Her work.

Walking in the Spirit, Praying in the Spirit, Hearing in the Spirit, Seeing in the Spirit, Fighting in the Spirit, Worshipping in the Spirit, and ultimately Living in the Spirit are all directly connected. We are all as <u>one</u> in the Spirit when we are one <u>with</u> The Spirit... in the One Body of Christ.

The following Scriptures primarily focus on, and give us examples of, Walking in the Spirit.

### John 14:23,26

*Jesus replied, "Anyone who loves Me will obey My teaching. My Father will love them, and We will All come to them and make Our home with them. But **the Comforter, the Holy Spirit**, whom the Father will send in My name, **She will teach you all things, and bring to your remembrance all things that I said to you.***"

### Romans 8:1-39

Paul writing: *There is, therefore now **no condemnation to those who** are in Christ Jesus, who do not <u>Walk</u> according to the Flesh, but **according to The Spirit**. For the Law of **the Spirit of Life** in Christ Jesus **has made me free** from the law of sin and death. For the Law was powerless, in that it was weak through the Flesh, but what GOD did by sending His own Son in the likeness of sinful Flesh, on account of sin, He condemned sin in the Flesh, that **the righteous requirement of the Law might be <u>fulfilled in us</u> <u>who do not Walk according to the Flesh, but Walk</u> <u>according to The Spirit</u>**. For those who live according to the Flesh set their minds on the things of the Flesh, but **those who live according to The Spirit, set their minds on the things of The Spirit**. For to be carnally minded is death, but to be spiritually minded is Life and Peace. Because the carnal mind is hostile against GOD; for it is not subject to the Law of GOD, nor indeed can be. So then, those who are in the Flesh cannot please GOD.*

***But you are not in the Flesh but in The Spirit, if indeed the Spirit of GOD dwells in you. Now, if anyone does not have the Spirit of the Messiah, they are not His*** (Jesus').

*But if Christ Jesus is in you, truly the body is dead because of sin, but your spirit is alive because of righteousness. Now, if The Spirit of the One who raised Jesus from the dead dwells in you, the One who raised Jesus, the Messiah, from the dead will also give Life to your mortal bodies, through His Spirit who dwells in you.*

*Since therefore, brothers and sisters, we are debtors – not to the Flesh, to live according to the Flesh. For if you live according to the Flesh you will die; but **if by The Spirit you put to death the deeds of the Flesh, you will live. <u>For as many as are Led by the Spirit of GOD, these are Children of GOD</u>.** For you did not receive the spirit of bondage again to fear, but **you have received the Spirit of Adoption**, by whom we cry out, "Abba, Father!" ("Daddy, Father!") <u>**The Spirit Herself Confirms with our spirit that we are Children of GOD, and if Children, then also heirs – heirs indeed of GOD and joint-heirs with the Messiah**</u>, if perhaps we suffer with Him, in order that we may also be glorified together.*

*For I have concluded that the sufferings of this present time are not worthy to be compared with the glory which shall be revealed in us. For the earnest expectation of the Creation eagerly waits for the disclosure of the sons of GOD. For the Creation was subjected to futility, not willingly, but because of the One who subjected it in hope; because the Creation itself also will be set free from the bondage of decay into the same glorious freedom as the Children of GOD, for we know that all of Creation groans and labors together with Birth Pains until now. Not only that, but **we also who have the First-Fruits of The Spirit**, even we ourselves grieve within us, eagerly waiting for the adoption, the redemption of our body. For we were saved in this hope, but hope that is seen is not hope; for why does one still hope for what he sees? However, if we hope for what we do not see, we eagerly wait for it patiently.*

Likewise, **_The Spirit also helps us in our weaknesses_**, *for we do not know what we should pray for as we need to, but* **_The Spirit Herself intercedes on our behalf_**, *crying out with words that cannot be expressed.  Now searching the deepest parts of our hearts,* **the purpose of The Spirit is known, because the intercession made by The Spirit for Believers is according to the Will of GOD.  And we know that all things work together for good to those who love GOD, to those who are the Called, according to the divine purpose.**  *For those known beforehand, were also predestined to be conformed to the image of His Son, that He* (Jesus) *might be the Firstborn among many brothers and sisters.  But, those predestined, these were also Called; those Called, these were also justified; and those justified, these were also glorified.*

*What then shall we say to these things?*  **If GOD is for us, who can be against us?**  *Indeed, He who did not spare His own Son, but delivered Him up for us all, how shall He not with Him also freely give us all things?  Who shall bring a charge against GOD's elect?  GOD is the One who justifies as guilty or innocent.  Who is the One who sentences?  It is Jesus, the Messiah, the One who died, and furthermore has been raised from the dead, and is also at the right-hand of God* (the Father)*, who also makes an appeal for us.  Who shall separate us from the Love of Christ?  Shall tribulation, or distress, or persecution, or famine, or nakedness, or danger, or sword?  As it is written:*

*"For Your sake, we are killed all day long; we are accounted as sheep for the slaughter."*

**Yet in all these things, we are more than conquerors through the One who loves us.**  *For I am persuaded that neither death nor life, nor Angels, nor Principalities, nor Powers, nor things present, nor things to come, nor height, nor depth, nor any other created thing;* **nothing shall be able to separate us from the Love of GOD, which is in Christ Jesus our Lord.**

*John 4:23-24*

Jesus speaking: *"But the hour is coming, and now is, when the **true worshipers will worship the Father in Spirit and Truth**, for the Father is seeking such to worship Him. **God** (the Father) **is Spirit, and those who worship Him must worship in Spirit and Truth."***

*Acts 7:55-56*

But **Stephen, being full of the Holy Spirit, looked up intently into Heaven, and saw the Glory of GOD,** *and Jesus standing at the right-hand of God* (the Father). *He said, "Behold, I see the Heavens open and the Son of Man standing at the right-hand of God."*

*Acts 10:19-20*

*While Peter was still thinking about his Vision, **the Holy Spirit said to him**, "Simon, three men are looking for you. So, get up and go downstairs. Do not hesitate to go with them, for I have sent them."*

*Acts 11:12-18*

Peter speaking: *"**The Holy Spirit told me** to have no hesitation about going with them. These six brothers also went with me, and we entered the man's house. He told us how he had seen an Angel appear in his house and say, 'Send to Joppa for Simon, who is called Peter. He will bring you a message through which you and all your household will be saved.' As I began to speak, **the Holy Spirit came on them as She had come on us at the beginning**. Then I remembered what the Lord Jesus had* *said: 'John baptized with water, but **you will be baptized with the Holy Spirit**.' So, if GOD gave them the same Gift that He gave us who believed in the Lord Jesus, the Messiah, who was I to think that I could stand in GOD's way?" When they heard this, they had no further objections and praised GOD, saying, "So then, even to Gentiles GOD has granted repentance that leads to Life."*

*Acts 15:22-33*

*Then the Apostles and Elders, with the whole Church, decided to choose some of their own men and send them to Antioch with Paul and Barnabas. They chose Judas – called Barsabbas – and Silas, men who were leaders among the Believers. With them, they sent the following letter:*

*"The Apostles and Elders, your brothers, to the Gentile Believers in Antioch, Syria, and Cilicia: Greetings. We have heard that some went out from us without our authorization and disturbed you, troubling your minds by what they said. So, we all agreed to choose some men and send them to you with our dear friends Barnabas and Paul, men who have risked their lives for the name of our Lord Jesus, the Messiah. Therefore, we are sending Judas and Silas to confirm by word of mouth what we are writing. **It seemed good to the Holy Spirit** and to us not to burden you with anything beyond the following requirements: You are to abstain from food sacrificed to Idols, from blood, from the meat of strangled animals, and from sexual immorality. You will do well to avoid these things. Farewell."*

*So the men were sent off and went down to Antioch, where they gathered the Church together and delivered the letter. The people read it and were glad for its encouraging* *message.  **Judas and Silas, who themselves were Prophets, said much to encourage and strengthen the Believers.** After spending some time there, they were sent off by the Believers with the blessing of Peace to return to those who had sent them.*

### Acts 16:6-10

***Paul and his companions** traveled throughout the region of Phrygia and Galatia, **having been prevented by the Holy Spirit from preaching the Word in the province of Asia**, they then came down to the border of Mysia and **tried to enter Bithynia, but the Spirit of Jesus would not allow them to**.  So, they passed by Mysia and went down to Troas.  **During the night, Paul had a Vision of a man of Macedonia standing and begging him, "Come over to Macedonia and help us."**  After Paul had seen the Vision, we got ready at once to leave for Macedonia, **concluding that GOD had Called us to preach the Gospel to them**.*

### Acts 19:21

*When these things were accomplished, **Paul, in the Spirit, had an idea placed within him**, that when he had passed through Macedonia and Achaia, to go to Jerusalem, saying, **"After I have been there, I must also see Rome."***

### Acts 20:22-28

Paul speaking to the Church Leaders:  ***"And now, compelled by The Spirit, I am going to Jerusalem, not knowing what will happen to me there.  I only know that in every city, the Holy Spirit warns me that chains and persecution await me**.  However, I consider my life worth* *nothing to me; my only aim is to finish the race and complete the task the Lord Jesus has given me – the task of testifying to the Gospel of GOD's Grace.* **Now I know that none of you among whom I have gone about preaching The Kingdom will ever see me again.** *Therefore, I declare to you today that I am innocent of the blood of any of you, for I have not hesitated to declare to you the whole counsel of GOD.* **Keep watch over yourselves and all the flock** (of Believers) *of which* **the Holy Spirit has made you overseers, to shepherd the Church of GOD,** *which was purchased with the Blood of Her own Son.*

(The Holy Spirit was emphasizing through Paul of the Leaders' great responsibility to care for Her Children, because of the high price that was paid by Her Son)

## Acts 21:4-11

*We sought out the Disciples there and stayed with them for seven days.* **Through The Spirit, they urged Paul not to go on to Jerusalem.** *After we had been there a number of days,* **a Prophet named Agabus** *came down from Judea. Coming over to us, he took Paul's belt, tied his own hands and feet with it, and said,* **"The Holy Spirit says, 'In this way, the Jewish leaders in Jerusalem will bind the owner of this belt and will hand him over to the Gentiles.'"**

## Romans 14:14-23

*I know and am convinced that in the Lord Jesus that there is nothing unclean of itself; but to the one who considers anything to be unclean, to them, it is unclean. Yet* **if your brother or sister is grieved because of your food, you are no longer Walking in Love.** *Do not destroy with your food*

218

or drink the one for whom the Messiah died.  Therefore, do not let your good be spoken of as evil; for **the Kingdom of GOD is** not eating and drinking, but **righteousness and Peace and Joy in the Holy Spirit**.  For the one who serves the Messiah in this is very pleasing to GOD and approved by men.  So therefore, **let us pursue the things which make for Peace and the things by which one may build up another**.  Do not destroy the work of GOD for the sake of food or drink.  All things indeed are pure, but it is evil for the man who eats or drinks, knowing he is offending another.  **It is good neither to eat meat nor drink wine nor do anything by which causes your brother or sister to stumble, or be led into sin or become weak.**  You that have Faith, have it to yourself before GOD.  Blessed is the one who does not condemn themselves in what they approve.  However, **the one who doubts is condemned if** they eat or drink, because **they do not do it out of Faith; for whatever is _not_ done out of Faith, is sin.**

### 1 Corinthians 3:1-17

And I, brothers and sisters, could not speak to you as to spiritual people, but as to carnal, as to infants in the Messiah.  I fed you with Milk and not with solid food; for you were not able to receive it.  In fact, even now, you are still not able, for you are still carnal.  **For where there are jealousy and strife among you, are you not carnal and Walking according to man?**  For when one says, "I am of Paul," and another, "I am of Apollos," are you not carnal?  Who then is Apollos?  Who is Paul?  Servants through whom you believed, even as the Lord has given to each one.  I planted, Apollos watered, but GOD caused it to grow.  So then neither he who plants is anything, nor he who waters, but only the One who causes it to grow – GOD.  Now he who plants and he who waters are one, and each one will

219

*receive his own reward according to his own labor.* **For we are GOD's fellow workers; we are GOD's field, we are GOD's building.**

*According to the Grace of GOD, which was given to me, as a wise master builder, I have laid the foundation, and another builds on it. But let each one take heed how he builds on it,* **for no one can lay any foundation other than the One already laid, which is Jesus, the Messiah.** *Now if anyone builds on this foundation with gold, silver, precious stones, wood, hay, or straw, each one's work will become apparent; for the Day will reveal it, because it will be brought into the light by Fire; and the Fire will Test each one's work, of what manner it is. If anyone's work which he has built on it endures, he will receive a reward. If anyone's work is burned, he will suffer loss; but he himself will be saved, yet so as through Fire.*

**<u>Do you not know that you yourselves are the Temple of GOD and that the Spirit of GOD dwells in you?</u> If anyone destroys the Temple of GOD, GOD will destroy him. For the Temple of GOD is holy, which you are.**

### 1 Corinthians 6:9-20
*Do you not know that the unrighteous will not inherit the Kingdom of GOD? Do not be deceived. Neither the sexually immoral, nor Idol-worshippers, nor adulterers, nor those who allow or enable homosexuality, nor homosexuals, nor thieves, nor covetous, nor drunkards, nor abusive, nor greedy swindlers will inherit the Kingdom of GOD. And such were some of you.* **<u>But you were washed, but you were sanctified, but you were justified in the name of the Lord Jesus and by the Spirit of our GOD.</u>**

*All things are lawful for me, but all things are not helpful.*

*All things are lawful for me, but I will not be controlled by anything. Foods for the stomach and the stomach for foods, but GOD will destroy both it and them. Now the body is not for sexual immorality but for the Lord, and the Lord for the body.* **And GOD both raised up the Lord and will also raise us up by His Power.** *Do you not know that your bodies are members of Christ? Shall I then take the members of Christ and make them members of a prostitute? Certainly not! Or do you not know that he who is joined to a prostitute is one body with her? For the LORD GOD says,* **"The two shall become one flesh."** *So, he who is joined to the LORD GOD, is one spirit with the LORD GOD.*

*Flee sexual immorality. Every sin that a man does is outside the body, but he who commits sexual immorality sins against his own body.* ***<u>Or do you not know that your body is the Temple of the Holy Spirit who is in you, whom you have from GOD, and you are not your own? For you were bought at a price; therefore, glorify GOD in your body and in your spirit, which are both GOD's.</u>***

<u>*2 Corinthians 11:1-15*</u>
*I hope you will bear with me in a little foolishness, and indeed you bear with me. I am jealous for you with a Godly jealousy. I promised you in marriage to One Husband, so that I might present you as a pure Virgin to Christ. However, I am afraid that just as Eve was deceived by the serpent's trickery, your minds may somehow be corrupted from your sincerity and purity in Christ.* **For if someone comes to you and preaches another Jesus, other than the Jesus we preached, or if you receive a different spirit from The Spirit you received, or a different gospel from the one you accepted, you tolerate it easily enough.** *I do not think I am in the least inferior to those other most distinguished Apostles. I may indeed be unpolished as a*

*speaker, but not in Knowledge. We have made all things perfectly clear to you in every way. Or was it a sin for me to lower myself in order to elevate you by preaching the Gospel of GOD to you free of charge? I robbed other Churches by receiving support from them so as to serve you. And when I was with you and needed something, I was not a burden to anyone, for the brothers who came from Macedonia supplied what I needed. I have kept myself from being a burden to you in any way, and will continue to do so. As surely as the Truth of Christ is in me, nobody in the regions of Achaia will stop this boasting of mine. Why? Because I do not love you? GOD knows I do! And I will keep on doing what I am doing in order to cut the ground from under those who want an opportunity to be considered equal with us in the things they boast about, for such people are false apostles, deceitful workers, masquerading as apostles of Christ. And no wonder, for Satan himself masquerades as an Angel of light. It is not surprising, then, if his servants also masquerade as servants of righteousness. Their end will be what their actions deserve.*

### 2 Corinthians 13:11-14
*Finally, brothers and sisters, rejoice! Strive for full restoration, encourage one another, be of one mind, live in Peace. And the GOD of Love and Peace will be with you. Greet one another with a holy kiss. All GOD's people here send their greetings. May the Grace of the Lord Jesus, the Messiah, and the Love of GOD, and the fellowship of the Holy Spirit be with you all.*

*Galatians 4:28-31*

*Now you, brothers and sisters, like Isaac was, are Children of Promise.* ***But, just as then, he who was born according to the Flesh persecuted him who was born according to The Spirit, so it is now.*** *However, what does the Scripture say? "Cast out the slave woman and her son, for the son of the slave woman shall not share in the inheritance with the son of the free woman."* ***So then, brothers and sisters, we are not children of the slave woman, but of the free Woman*** (Holy Spirit).


*Galatians 5:1-25*

*For freedom,* ***the Messiah has set us free.*** *Stand firm, therefore, and do not let yourselves be entangled again by a yoke of slavery. Mark my words! Behold, I Paul say to you that if you now become circumcised, Christ will not benefit you at all. Again,* ***I declare to every man who now becomes circumcised*** (or decides to follow any of the Old Testament "Laws") ***is a debtor, and he is obligated to obey the whole Law. You who are trying to be justified by the Law have been alienated from Christ; for you have fallen away from Grace.*** *For we, through The Spirit by Faith,* ***eagerly await the Hope of righteousness.*** *For in Christ Jesus, neither circumcision nor uncircumcision counts for anything; but only Faith expressing itself through Love. You were running the race well. Who hindered you, to keep you from obeying the Truth?* ***That belief does not come from the One calling you.*** *"A little yeast will leaven the whole lump of dough." I am confident in the Lord that you will not have any other thoughts like these. The one, however, who is troubling you, whoever that may be, will have to pay the penalty. Now brothers and sisters, if I am still preaching circumcision, why am I still being persecuted? In that case, the offense of the cross has been abolished. As for those agitators, I wish they would go the whole way, cut it off, and emasculate themselves!*

*You, my brothers and sisters, were called to be free. But do not use your freedom to indulge the Flesh. Instead, serve one another through Love.* **For the entire Law is fulfilled in keeping this one Command: "Love your neighbor as yourself."** *If you bite and devour each other, watch out, or you will be destroyed by one another.*

*Now I say,* <u>Walk by The Spirit, and you will not gratify the desires of the Flesh.</u> **For the Flesh desires what is contrary to The Spirit, and The Spirit, what is contrary to the Flesh. They are in opposition to each other so that you do not do just whatever you happen to desire. However,** <u>**if you are Led by The Spirit, you are not under the Law.**</u> *The acts of the Flesh are evident: which are sexual immorality, impurity, debauchery, idolatry, witchcraft, hatred, strife, jealousy, outbursts of anger, rivalries, rebellions, factions, envyings, drunkenness, orgies, and other things like these. I warn you, as I did before, that those who do these things will not inherit the Kingdom of GOD.* **But** <u>**the fruit of The Spirit is Love, Joy, Peace, patience, kindness, goodness, faithfulness, gentleness, and self-control**</u>. *Against such things, there is no law. Those who belong to Christ Jesus have crucified the Flesh with its passions and desires.* <u>*If we Live by The Spirit, we should also Walk by The Spirit.*</u>


<u>*Galatians 6:1-10*</u>
**Brothers and sisters, even if someone is trapped in sin,** <u>**you who Live by The Spirit**</u> **should restore that person in a spirit of gentleness, but consider yourself, or you may also be tempted. Carry each other's burdens, and in this way, you will fulfill the Law of Christ. If anyone thinks they are someone important, when they are not, they deceive themselves. Each one should examine their own actions. Then they can take pride in themselves alone, without**

*comparing themselves to someone else, for each one should carry their own load. Nevertheless, the one who receives instruction in the Word should share all good things with their Instructor.* ***Do not be deceived; GOD is not mocked. For whatever a man sows, that he will also reap.*** *Whoever sows to their Flesh, from the flesh will reap destruction.* ***However, whoever sows to The Spirit, from The Spirit will reap Eternal Life. Let us not become weary in doing good, for at the proper time we will reap a harvest, if we do not give up. Therefore accordingly, as we have an opportunity, let us do good to all people, especially to those Believers who belong to the family of our Faith.***

<u>*Ephesians 4:17-32*</u>

*This I say, therefore, and testify in the Lord, that you should no longer walk as the rest of the Gentiles walk, in the futility of their mind, having their understanding darkened, being alienated from the life of GOD, because of the ignorance that is in them, because of the blindness of their heart; who, being past feeling, have given themselves over to lewdness, to work all uncleanness with greediness.*

*But you have not so learned the Messiah, if indeed you have heard Him and have been taught by Him, as the Truth is in Jesus:* ***that you put off, concerning your former conduct, the old man which grows corrupt according to the deceitful lusts, and be*** <u>***renewed in the spirit of your mind,***</u> ***and that*** <u>***you put on the New Man which was created***</u> ***according to GOD, in true righteousness and holiness.***

***Therefore, you must stop telling lies, "Let each one of you speak Truth with his neighbor," for we are members of the same Body.*** <u>***"Be angry, but do not sin": do not let the sun go down on your anger, nor give an Open Door to the Devil to come in.***</u> *Let him who stole steal no longer, but* *rather let him labor, working with his hands what is good, that he may have something to give him who has need.* **Let no corrupt word proceed out of your mouth***, but what is good for necessary edification, that it may impart Grace to the hearers.* **And <u>do not grieve the Holy Spirit of GOD</u>, by whom you were sealed for the day of redemption. Let all bitterness, wrath, anger, loud arguing, and evil speaking be put away from you, along with all wickedness. And be kind to one another, tenderhearted, forgiving one another, even as GOD in the Messiah forgave you.**

## *Ephesians 5:1-21*

**Therefore be imitators of GOD, as beloved Children, and Walk in Love, just as the Messiah also has loved us and gave Himself for us as an offering and sacrifice to GOD of a sweet-smelling aroma.** *However, sexual immorality and all impurity or covetousness, let it not even be named among you, as is proper among Believers; neither filthiness, nor foolish talking, nor coarse crude joking, which are not fitting, but rather giving of thanks. For you may be sure of this, that everyone who is sexually immoral or impure, or who is covetous – that is an Idolater – has no inheritance in the Kingdom of the Messiah and GOD. Let no one deceive you with empty words, for because of these things, the Wrath of GOD comes upon the sons of disobedience. Therefore, do not be partakers with them.*

*For you were once darkness, but now you are light in the Lord;* **Walk as Children of light – for the fruit of the light is in all goodness, righteousness, and truth – discerning what is acceptable to the Lord.** *And have no fellowship with the unfruitful works of darkness, but rather expose them. For it is shameful even to speak of those things which are done by them in secret. But all things that are exposed are made visible by the light, for whatever becomes visible is light.*

*Therefore, He says:*

*"Awake, you who sleep, arise from the dead, and the Messiah will shine light upon you."*

*See then that you Walk carefully, not as fools, but as wise, redeeming the time, because the days are evil.  Therefore, do not be foolish, but **understand what the Will of the Lord is.  And <u>do not be drunk with wine</u>, in which is depravity; but instead, <u>be filled with The Spirit</u>, speaking to one another in psalms and hymns and spiritual songs, singing and making melody in your heart to the Lord, giving thanks always for all things to God the Father, in the name of our Lord Jesus, the Messiah, submitting to one another in the Reverence of the Messiah.***

*Philippians 2:1-4*
***Therefore if there is** any encouragement in Christ, if any Comfort of love, if **any fellowship of The Spirit**, if any affections and compassions, **fulfill my Joy by being like-minded, having the same love, being of one accord, of one mind, letting nothing be done through selfish ambition or vain conceit, but in humility let each consider others above themselves.  Let each of you look out not only for your own interests, but also for the interests of others.***

*Philippians 3:1-3*
*Finally, my brothers and sisters, rejoice in the Lord.  For me to write the same things to you is not tedious, but for you, it brings security.  Beware of dogs, beware of evil workers, beware of the false circumcision!* (followers of the Law)  ***<u>For we are</u> the circumcision,** (true Believers) **<u>who worship GOD in the Spirit</u>, rejoice in Christ Jesus, and have no confidence in the Flesh.***

*1 Thessalonians 5:16-22*
*__Rejoice always, pray without ceasing, in everything give__*
*__thanks; for this is the Will of GOD in Christ Jesus for you.__*
*__Do not quench The Spirit.  Do not despise Prophecies.__*
*__Test all things; hold fast to what is good.  Abstain from__*
*__every form of evil.__*


*1 Timothy 4:1-5*
*Now __The Spirit clearly states that in the Last Days some__*
*__will depart from the Faith__, paying attention to deceiving*
*spirits and the instructions of Demons, speaking lies in*
*hypocrisy, whose consciences have been seared, so they*
*no longer feel, who forbid marriage and require*
*abstinence from foods that GOD created to be received*
*with thanksgiving by those who believe and know the*
*Truth.  For everything created by GOD is good, and*
*nothing is to be rejected if it is received with thanksgiving,*
*for it is made holy by the Word of GOD and prayer.*


*James 4:1-10*
*Where do disputes and fights come from among you?  Do*
*they not come from the desires and lust of the Flesh that*
*you fight within your body?  You lust after and do not have.*
*You murder and become envious but cannot obtain; you*
*argue and fight.  __You do not have because you do not ask.__*
*__You ask and do not receive, because you ask wrongly, that__*
*__you may spend it on your pleasures.__  Adulterers and*
*adulteresses!  Do you not know that friendship with the*
*world is hostility with GOD?  Whoever therefore wants to*
*be a friend of the world makes himself an adversary of*
*GOD.  Or do you think that the Scripture says in vain,*
*__"The Spirit who dwells in us yearns jealously for our__*
*__relationship."__?  But we are given more Grace.  Therefore*

*the Scripture also says:* **"G**OD** resists the proud, but gives Grace to the humble."**

**Therefore, <u>submit yourselves to G</u>**OD**<u>; resist the Devil, and he will flee from you. Draw near to G</u>**OD**<u>, and G</u>**OD** <u>will draw near to you.</u>** *Cleanse your hands, you sinners, and purify your hearts, you double-minded. Grieve and mourn and weep!* Let your laughter be turned to mourning and your Joy to gloom. **Humble yourselves in the presence of the L**ORD**, and you will be raised up.**

### *1 John 3:16-4:7*

*By this we come to know what Love is, that Jesus laid down His life for us, and **we ought to lay down our lives for our brothers and sisters**.* *But whoever of you has the wealth of this world and sees his brother in need, yet closes his heart against him, how does G*OD*'s Love reside in him? Little children, let us not only love in words or speech, but in deeds and in truth. And by this, we shall know that we are of the Truth, and before Him will assure our heart, for whenever our heart condemns us, G*OD* is greater than our heart, and knows all things. Beloved, if our heart does not condemn us, we have assurance before G*OD*; and whatever we ask we receive from Him, because we keep His Commandments and do what pleases Him. And **<u>this is His Commandment, that we Believe in the name of His Son Jesus, the Messiah, and we should love one another, just as He has commanded us.</u>** Whoever keeps His Commandments resides in Him, and He in them. And <u>**by this, we know that He resides in us, by The Spirit who has been given to us.**</u>*

**Beloved, do not believe every spirit, but Test the spirits to see whether they are from G**OD**, because many false prophets have gone out into the world. By this, you know the Spirit of G**OD**: Every spirit that confesses that Jesus is**

the Messiah, and has come in the flesh, is from GOD, and every spirit that does not confess Jesus, the Messiah, has come in the flesh, is not from GOD. This is the spirit of the antichrist, which you heard was coming and now is in the world already. _Little Children, you are from GOD and have overcome them, for the One who is in you_ (The Holy Spirit) _is greater than the one_ (the Devil and his minions) _who is in the world._ They are of the world; therefore, they speak from the world, and the world listens to them. We are from GOD. Whoever knows GOD listens to us; whoever is not from GOD does not listen to us. _By this, we know the Spirit of Truth and the spirit of deception._

_Jude 1:17-23_

But you, beloved, must remember the words spoken beforehand by the Apostles of our Lord Jesus, the Messiah, that they said to you, "In the End Times (Last Days) there will be scoffers, following after their own ungodly passions." It is these who cause strife and division, worldly-minded people, not having The Spirit in them. _But you, beloved, build yourselves up in your most holy Faith and pray in the Holy Spirit, keeping yourselves in the Love of GOD,_ waiting for the Mercy of our Lord Jesus, the Messiah that leads to Eternal Life. And have mercy on those who have doubts; save others by snatching them out of the fire; to others show mercy with respect, hating even the garments that have been stained by the Flesh.

## Revelation 1:1-11

*The Revelation of Jesus, the Messiah, which God* (the Father) *gave Him to show His servants, the things which must shortly take place. And He sent and signified it by His Angel to His servant John, who bore witness to the Word of GOD, and to the testimony of Jesus Christ, to all things that he saw. Blessed is he who reads and those who hear the words of this Prophecy, and keep those things which are written in it; for the time is near.*

*John, **to the Seven Churches** (all the Churches) which are in Asia: Grace to you and Peace **from Him** (the Father) who is and who was and who is to come, and **from the Seven Spirits** (the Holy Spirit) who are before His Throne, and **from Jesus Christ** (the Son), the faithful witness, the Firstborn from the dead, and the ruler over the kings of the Earth. To Him who loved us and washed us from our sins in His own Blood, and has made us Royalty, priests to His God and Father, to Him be Glory and dominion forever and ever. Amen. Behold, He* (Jesus) *is coming with the clouds, and every eye will see Him, even they who pierced Him. And all the Tribes of the Earth will mourn because of Him. Even so, Amen. "I am the Alpha and the Omega, the Beginning and the End," says The LORD GOD, "who is and who was and who is to come, the Almighty."*

*I, John, both your brother and companion in the Tribulation and Kingdom and patience of Jesus, the Messiah, was on the island that is called Patmos for the Word of GOD and for the testimony of Jesus Christ. **I was in the Spirit on the Lord's Day**, and I heard behind me a loud voice, as of a trumpet, saying, "I am the Alpha and the Omega, the First and the Last," and, "What you see, write in a book and send it to the Seven Churches which are in Asia: to Ephesus, to Smyrna, to Pergamos, to Thyatira, to Sardis, to Philadelphia, and to Laodicea."*

# CHAPTER EIGHTEEN

# THE HOLY SPIRIT: TESTS US

Testing is a topic that most avoid, while others try hard not to even discuss. It involves the second part in the role as our Teacher by the Holy Spirit. You see, once a Teacher has taught a lesson in school, we get "Tested". Being Tested is not enjoyable, but it can be very revealing, not only to the Teacher, but more importantly, to the student. Jesus was even Tested, but He had to endure even more severe Testing than we have ever, or will ever have to undergo.

Our own Testing, however, is similar to what most Believers endure. We are taught certain things, and then the Holy Spirit will see if we learned the lesson, truly believe what we say that we believe, and are willing to apply the lesson to our lives. Sometimes we pass the Test, then move on to the next lesson, but at other times, we fail and must repeat the lesson until we pass. I have seen this occur so many times, not only with myself, but so many others around me. This Testing plays an essential role in our spiritual development. My advice for you is that you learn from your failures, but keep moving forward, and just don't give up.

*Mark 1:9-13*
*It came to pass in those days that Jesus came from Nazareth of Galilee, and was baptized by John in the Jordan River. And immediately, coming up from the water, He saw the Heavens open up, and **The Spirit descend upon Him**, like a dove. Then a voice came from Heaven, "You are My Son, the beloved, in You, I am well pleased." Immediately, **The Spirit drove Him into the wilderness**. And He was there in the wilderness forty days, **Tested by Satan**, and was with the wild beasts; and the Angels ministered to Him.*

## Luke 4:1-2

*Now __filled with the Holy Spirit__, Jesus returned from the Jordan River. And then __The Spirit led Him into the desert. There the Devil Tested__ Jesus for 40 days. Jesus ate nothing during this time, and when it was finished, he was very hungry.*

## Luke 8:13

Jesus speaking: *"And the ones on the rock are those who, when they hear the Word, receive it with Joy. But __because these have no roots, they believe for a while, and in time of Testing, they fall away__."*

## John 16:33

Jesus speaking: *"I have told you all this so that you may have Peace in Me. __Here on Earth you will have many Trials__ (Tests) __and sorrows__. But take heart, because I have overcome the world."*

## 1 Peter 4:12-19

*__Beloved, do not be surprised at the fiery Trial when it comes upon you to Test you, as though something strange was happening to you.__ But rejoice to the extent that you share Christ's sufferings, that you may also rejoice and be glad when His Glory is revealed. __If you are insulted in the name of Christ, you are blessed, because the Glory and the Spirit of GOD rests upon you.__ But let none of you suffer as a murderer or a thief or an evildoer or as a meddler. __Yet if anyone suffers as a Christian, let him not be ashamed, but let him glorify GOD in that name.__ For it is time for judgment to begin at the household of GOD; and* *if it begins with us, what will be the outcome for those who do not obey the Gospel of GOD? And, "If the righteous is scarcely saved, what will become of the ungodly and the sinner?"* **Therefore, let those who suffer according to GOD's Will entrust their Souls to a faithful Creator while doing good.**

### Romans 5:3-5
**We can rejoice, too, when we run into problems and Trials, for we know that they help us develop Endurance. And Endurance develops strength of Character, and Character strengthens our confident Hope of salvation. And this Hope will not lead to disappointment. For we know how dearly God the Father loves us, because He has given us the Holy Spirit to fill our hearts with Their Love.**

### Romans 12:2
*Do not be conformed to this world, but be transformed by the renewing of your mind,* **that by Testing you may discern what the good and acceptable and perfect Will of GOD is.**

### 1 Corinthians 10:13-14
**No Trial has overtaken you except such as is common to man; but GOD is faithful, who will not allow you to be Tested beyond what you are able, but with the Trial will also make the way of Escape, that you may be able to endure it.**

*2 Corinthians 1:3-7*

*Blessed be the God and Father of our Lord Jesus Christ,
the Father of mercies and **God of all Comfort, <u>who</u>
<u>comforts us in all our suffering, that we may be able to</u>
<u>comfort those who are in any distress, with the same</u>
<u>comfort with which we ourselves are comforted by God</u>**.
For as the sufferings of the Messiah abound in us, so our
comfort also abounds through Christ. Now if we are
afflicted, it is for your comfort and salvation, **which is
effective for enduring the same sufferings which we also
suffer**. Or if we are comforted, it is for your comfort and
salvation. And our hope for you is steadfast, because we
know that as you share in the sufferings, so also you will
share in the comfort.*

*1 Thessalonians 2:4*

*But just as we have been approved by GOD to be entrusted
with the Gospel, so we speak, not to please man, but to
please **<u>GOD, who Tests our hearts</u>**.*

*James 1:2-4, 12*

**<u>Count it all Joy, my brothers and sisters, when you fall</u>
<u>into Trials of various kinds, for you know that the Testing</u>
<u>of your Faith produces steadfastness</u>. And let
steadfastness have its full effect, that you may be mature
and complete, lacking in nothing. Blessed is the man who
remains steadfast under Trial, for when he has stood the
Test, he will receive the Crown of Life, which GOD has
promised to those who love Him.**

## 1 Peter 1:6-7

*In this, you can rejoice; there is wonderful Joy ahead,*
***even though you must endure many Trials for a little***
***while. These Trials will show that your Faith is genuine.***
*It is being Tested as Fire Tests and purifies gold – though*
*your Faith is far more precious than mere gold. So, when*
*your Faith remains strong through many Trials, it will*
*bring you much praise and glory and honor on the Day*
*when Jesus, the Messiah, is revealed to the whole world.*


## Hebrews 12:1-11

*Therefore we also, since we are surrounded by so great a*
*cloud of witnesses, let us lay aside every weight and the sin*
*which so easily ensnares us, and **let us run with endurance***
***the race that is set before us, looking unto Jesus**, the*
*Author and Finisher of our Faith, who for the Joy that was*
*set before Him **endured the cross, despising the shame**,*
*and has sat down at the right-hand of the Throne of GOD.*
*For consider Him who endured such hostility from sinners*
*against Himself, so you don't become weary and*
*discouraged in your Souls. You have not yet resisted to*
*bloodshed, striving against sin. And you have forgotten the*
*exhortation which speaks to you as to sons: **"My son, do***
***not despise the disciplining of the LORD, nor be***
***discouraged when you are corrected by Him; for whom***
***the Lord loves He disciplines**, and whips every son whom*
***He receives." If you endure the disciplining, GOD deals***
***with you as with sons; for what son is there whom a***
***father does not discipline? But if you are without***
***discipline, of which all have become partakers, then you***
***are illegitimate and not sons. Furthermore, we have had***
*human fathers who corrected us, and we paid them respect.*
***Shall we not much more readily be in subjection to the***
***Father of spirits and Live?** For they indeed for a few days*
*disciplined us as seemed best to them, but He for our profit,*
*that we may be partakers of His Holiness. Now **no***

*discipline seems to be joyful for the present, but painful; nevertheless, afterward, it yields the peaceable fruit of righteousness to those who have been trained by it.*

*Deuteronomy 8:1-5*
Moses speaking: *"The whole commandment that I command you today you shall be careful to do, that you may live and multiply, and go in and possess the land that the LORD swore to give to your fathers. And you shall remember the whole way that the LORD your GOD has led you these forty years in the wilderness, that He might humble you, Testing you to know what was in your heart, whether you would keep His Commandments or not. And he humbled you and let you hunger and fed you with Manna, which you did not know, nor did your fathers know, that he might make you know that man does not live by bread alone, but man lives by every word that comes from the mouth of the LORD. Your clothing did not wear out on you and your foot did not swell these forty years. Know then in your heart that, just as a man disciplines his son, the LORD your GOD disciplines you."*

*Proverbs 17:3*
*Fire Tests the purity of silver and gold, but the LORD Tests the heart.*

Remember earlier when I said that when gold is refined, it must be heated with Fire until it has melted. Then the impurities float to the top where they can be seen and removed. In this same way, "Testing" helps us to be able to see our "impurities" or "baggage" and other issues within our Souls that hinder us from Walking with GOD. Our Trials by Fire help us understand who we are, and what may be hindering our Walk, so it then can be skimmed off and removed from our hearts.

238

# CHAPTER NINETEEN

# THE HOLY SPIRIT:
## LOVES, COMFORTS, & NURTURES US

We will now look at the more tender side of the Holy Spirit. Ever since my life as a Child of GOD began, that is, my life as a Christian Believer, I can say without hesitation that I have felt Her Love, Comfort, and Nurturing regularly. I would often describe it like having loving arms wrapped around me and being covered with warm liquid love that just washes over me and envelopes me. It can be hard to put words to these feelings, but She knows very well how to make Her Children feel loved. That love extends from the Father, and Jesus as well, but I have genuinely felt a "Mother's Love" from Her that is unique.

There have also been times in my life when She has allowed me to feel Her personal feelings about something, whether it was Her Love for me, or for someone else, or Her feelings about something that She was grieving about, like Her Children being slaughtered in other Countries. During these times that She had shared Her feelings with me, I have been overwhelmed by the emotions, and it brought me to my knees. The sheer volume of Her emotions would overflow within me, as tears began to run down my face, almost as if She were crying through me. I cannot describe it any other way except to say that I was filled with emotions that were not mine, and at a level that I have never felt or experienced, other than from Her. I believe this is where people have come up with the expression, "GOD is Love!" because they have felt the Love of GOD through their relationship with the Holy Spirit. Yes, GOD is Love, but GOD expresses many, many other emotions, just like us, or instead, ours are just like Theirs, since we were essentially *created in the Image and Likeness of GOD*.

So always remember this… as a Child of GOD, you are never alone; GOD is in you – all Three of Them – and They love you very much! Their love is without limits and is without condition. They are always there to Comfort you, Hold you, Love you, Nurture you, and Console you. They never sleep, and are always available. The Holy Spirit is the primary One that fulfills this role, as the Mother in the GODHEAD. You will be amazed at how you experience the Love of GOD once you see Her in this way. She has always been there, but She has just been misrepresented all these years. These are some of the Scriptures that focus on this topic, although some have already been given in previous Chapters, they are worth revisiting.

*John 14:16-17*

Jesus speaking: *"And I will ask the Father, and another* ***Comforter will be given to you, that will stay with you forever – the Spirit of Truth, whom the world is not able to receive, because it neither sees Her, nor knows Her; but you know Her, for She resides with you, and will be in you."***

*John 14:23,26*

*Jesus replied, "Anyone who loves Me will obey My teaching.* ***My Father will love them, and We will All come to them and make Our home with them. But the Comforter, the Holy Spirit, whom the Father will send in My name, She will teach you all things, and bring to your remembrance all things that I said to you."***

## John 15:26 - 16:15

Jesus speaking: *"**When the Comforter comes, whom I shall send to you from the Father, the Spirit of Truth who proceeds from the Father, She will testify of Me.** And you also bear witness, because you have been with Me from the beginning. These things I have spoken to you so that you will not stumble and fall away. They will put you out of the Churches and Synagogues, but the time is coming that whoever kills you will think they are offering service to GOD. And **these things they will do, because they have not known the Father nor Me.** But these things I have told you, that when their time comes, you may remember that I told you of them. And these things I did not say to you at the beginning, because I was with you.*

*But now I go away to the One who sent Me, and none of you asks Me, 'Where are You going?' But because I have said these things to you, sorrow has filled your heart. Nevertheless, **I tell you the truth, it is to your benefit that I go away; for if I do not go away, the Comforter will not come to you; but if I depart, I will send Her to you. And when She has come, She will convict the world concerning sin, and concerning righteousness, and concerning judgment: concerning sin, because they do not believe in Me; concerning righteousness, because I go to My Father and you see Me no more; concerning judgment, because the ruler of this world** (Satan) **has been judged. <u>I have so much more to tell you, but it is too much for you to accept now. But when the Spirit of Truth comes, She will lead you into all truth.</u> She will not speak of Herself, but whatever She hears, that She will speak, and will tell you what will happen in the future. She will glorify Me by telling you what She receives from Me. All that the Father possesses is Mine, that is why I said that the She will tell you what She receives from Me."***

*Acts 9:31*

Then **the Churches throughout** all *Judea, Galilee, and Samaria* **had Peace and were edified.** And <u>**Walking in the Reverence of the LORD and in the Comfort of the Holy Spirit**</u>, *they grew in number.*


*Romans 5:1-5*

*Therefore, since we have been justified through Faith, we have Peace with GOD through our Lord Jesus Christ, through whom we have gained access by Faith into this Grace in which we now stand. And we boast in the Hope of the Glory of GOD. Not only so, but we also glory in our Trials, because we know that Trials produce Endurance; Endurance, Character; and Character, Hope. And Hope does not put us to shame, because* **GOD's Love has been poured out into our hearts through the Holy Spirit, who has been given to us.**


*Romans 15:30-33*

**I urge you, brothers and sisters, by our Lord Jesus Christ and <u>by the Love of The Spirit</u>, to join me in my struggle by praying to GOD for me.** *Pray that I may be kept safe from the Unbelievers in Judea and that the contribution I take to Jerusalem may be favorably received by the Lord's people there, so that I may come to you with Joy, by GOD's Will, and in your company be refreshed. The GOD of Peace be with you all. Amen.*


*Colossians 1:1-18*

*Paul, an Apostle of Jesus, the Messiah, by the Will of GOD, and Timothy our brother, to the Believers and faithful brothers and sisters in Christ who are in Colossae:*

*Grace to you and Peace from God our Father.*

***We give thanks to the God and Father of our Lord Jesus Christ**, praying always for you, since we heard of your Faith in Christ Jesus and of your Love for all the Believers; because of the Hope which is laid up for you in the Heavens, of which you heard before in the Word of the Truth, the Gospel, the One who has come to you, just as it is also in all the world, bearing fruit and increasing, as it is also among you from the day you heard and knew the Grace of GOD in Truth; as you also learned from Epaphras, our beloved fellow bond-servant, who is a faithful minister of the Messiah on your behalf, **who also made known to us your Love in The Spirit**.*

*For this reason, we also, since the day we heard it, do not cease to pray for you, and to ask that you may be filled with the Knowledge of His* (the Father's) *Will in all spiritual Wisdom and Understanding; that you may Walk worthily of the Lord, fully pleasing Him, being fruitful in every good work and growing in the Knowledge of GOD; being strengthened with all Power, according to His glorious might, for all endurance and patience with Joy; giving thanks to **the Father** who has qualified us to be partakers of the inheritance of the Believers in the light. **He has rescued us from the dominion of darkness and transferred us into the Kingdom of the Son of His Love**, in whom we have redemption, the forgiveness of sins.*

***The Son is the image of the invisible GOD, the Firstborn of all Creation**. For by Him all things were created that are in the Heavens and upon the Earth, visible and invisible, whether thrones or dominions or Principalities or Powers. All things were created through Him and for Him. And He is before all things, and in Him all things are held together. And He is the Head of the Body, the Church, who is the beginning, the Firstborn from the dead, so that in all things He may have the preeminence.*

There is something that I wanted to point out to you about the Scriptures we just read in Colossians 1, from the previous page, that I think is interesting when I looked at this in the Greek. Keep in mind that this is in the context of all we have read up to this point. It would appear to me that the phrase "*the Son of His Love*" is actually referring to the "Son of the Father's Love"; which <u>could</u> really be referring to the "Son of the Holy Spirit". I am leaning towards this interpretation since there seems to be a clear difference in the way the Greek is worded here, from the way the Father said to Jesus in Luke 3:22, "*You are My beloved Son*". This is one of those Scriptures that makes me re-think what it's really saying, in the light of all we have just read up to this point.

This thought and feeling came to me when I was reading this in the original Greek. I just wanted to share the love I felt, that appeared to be from the Father, but was directed at His Wife, the Holy Spirit, The Queen.

Now that we have a new understanding of who the Holy Spirit is, and who She is not… all of the Old Testament and New Testament Scriptures come to life in a whole new way. I hope you have enjoyed Walking this out with me, so I wanted to finish up this journey with some of My Final Thoughts for you.

# CHAPTER TWENTY

# MY FINAL THOUGHTS

Since my initial Revelation about the Holy Spirit, and who She really is, I have come to have a deeper understanding of who the Father and Jesus are as well, and how They all interact. I now see that there are references in the Bible to each One of Them independently, as well as all three together as One GOD. I have also come to realize that They have three very unique voices and communicate with us very differently. When we are Born-Again, all three of Them will reside in us. And although They are all within us, the primary voice we will hear is that of the Holy Spirit. I have heard the voice of all three of Them, but primarily it has been the voice of the Holy Spirit. The two Verses below confirm this concept simply…

*John 14:23,26*
*Jesus replied, "Anyone who loves Me will obey My teaching. My Father will love them, and **We will All come to them and make Our home with them**. But the Comforter, the Holy Spirit, whom the Father will send in My name, **She will teach you all things**, and bring to your remembrance all things that I said to you."*

With all relationships, just like Theirs with us, we must each take the time to get to know Them as individuals, but also understand that They are One and have One voice as LORD GOD. Just as Jesus said, "*The LORD our GOD is One.*" I consider myself blessed to have received this Revelation, that I might share it with those of you who are reading this now, and that you would not only come to possess a deeper understanding about Them, but more importantly, come to have a closer relationship with Them because of it. The primary goal of anyone sharing their Faith with another should be to make the introduction, then simply help them grow in a direct relationship with GOD through the Holy Spirit. Our role is not to spoon-feed people _our_ Faith and have them dependent on us for their guidance. The best, most sincere, and purest Wisdom comes from GOD, not from man.

As I mentioned earlier, one thing that has helped me to get a clearer understanding of who They are, and who we are to Them, is to reflect upon this story – a story that originally came to me in the form of a Vision. It had several significant points, so I felt it's worth repeating, now that you have completed all the subsequent Chapters.

So, as you read it, let it sink deep into your heart…

As a young child, you suddenly find yourself walking through the forest of the most beautiful Kingdom you have ever seen, or even imagined could exist. Majestic mountains, green trees, endless colors of all types of flowers and birds, crystal clear streams of water flowing throughout the entire Kingdom, but seemingly coming from one direction, one Source. You walk towards the Source of the waters and come across the most incredible sight you have ever seen. There in the middle of this beautiful Paradise was a massive Castle. Now, this Castle is unlike anything you have ever seen or heard could even exist, and is so large that you cannot see the ends of it. As you walk towards one of its many gates, it opens for you on its own, as if it had been commanded to do so.

You walk inside, and everything you see has incredible designs and almost surreal architecture, and you wonder who could have designed and built such a place. As you continue to walk deeper and deeper inside, closer to the center, you see a grand Royal Palace in the middle of the Castle. You walk towards one of its jewel-covered doors, and as you look around, you are in awe of all you see, and yet again, the door opens on its own.

As you walk inside, you see hundreds of Ambassadors and Leaders from many Nations. They turn to see who just came through the door, as they all seem to see you at once. They all just stop speaking suddenly, then immediately begin to clear a path for you to the center of the room. As they move out of the way, you are amazed as you see three Regal Thrones, and sitting on them is the King, the Queen, and the Prince. Their eyes are fixed on you, and They all smile and open Their arms, gesturing for you to come to Them. As you slowly walk forward, you finally get close enough to Them, that the King and Queen grab you, lift you up in Their arms, place you on Their laps and say to you, "Welcome home My Child! We know that all this is new to you, and can be a little confusing, but you see, now that you have acknowledged Our Son, the Prince, as the One you are loyal to, you have become reborn into Our Kingdom and adopted as Our Child. You are now a joint heir to a royal inheritance and will be able to come to see us any time you wish. We will always be here for you, to love you, guide you, protect you, and care for you. We will teach you how to rule and exercise the Authority that We have granted you, which you now possess as Our Child. We will never leave you, and will always watch over you. You see, We have given Our Son, the Prince, to rule and be the King of kings and Lord of lords over the Earth and the Heavens above it. He has made a great sacrifice that you might live; no longer being subject to the Evil Ones of the Earth, but having Authority over them, since you are now royalty, being Our Child."

Then the King says, "We know that you will have many questions about how to walk in your new role as Our Child, and because the Prince knew He would have to return after His sacrifice, He asked Me to Promise to send the Queen to care for you all, which I have Promised Him. So, I have asked the Queen to go to the Earth and teach all of Our adopted Children everything you need to know about who Our Son the Prince is, what He has done for you, and about being royalty. She will also give you access to come to sit with Us at any time; We will hold you, love you, and teach you all you need to know. You have been granted access to Us any time you need to come to see Us. All those around Us will stop speaking, move out of the way, so you can come to the Throne any time you need to see Us. You are now royalty, one of Our Children, a prince or princess of the King, and the Queen will teach you how to walk in the Authority of the Prince, for He has been given dominion throughout all the Heavens and the Earth."

Here are a few Scriptures that confirm some of the concepts found in this Vision that I was shown:

*Hebrews 4:16*
*Let us, therefore, **come boldly to the Throne of Grace**, that we may obtain Mercy and find Grace to help in time of need.*

*John 14:16-17*
Jesus speaking: *"And I will ask the Father, and another **Comforter will be given to you, that will stay with you forever** – the Spirit of Truth, whom the world is not able to*

*receive, because it neither sees Her nor knows Her; but you*
*know Her, **for She resides with you, and will be in you**.*"


*Ephesians 2:18,22*
*For **through Him** (Jesus)**, we all have access in One Spirit***
***to the Father**. In Him you also are being built together*
*into a dwelling place for GOD by The Spirit.*


I love this story I was shown because it gives such a clear illustration of the relationship that we have with our sovereign LORD GOD, and shows us plainly that the Kingdom of GOD is a true Monarchy. The King is our Father God, the Queen is our Mother God (*the Holy Spirit*), and the Prince is God the Son, and our Lord Jesus – who in fact is our "Lord" because He has been given dominion and rule over the Heavens and the Earth by His Father, ever since He took back control over what Adam and Eve had given away to the Evil Ones. Once we accept the Gift and Sacrifice that Their Son Jesus made, by shedding His precious Blood, dying in our place, and providing us with a Pardon for our crimes against GOD, we then become Born-Again into our new life as a true Child of GOD, and adopted in by the Royal Family. Our Heavenly Parents have a love for us that is always there. And, since we are Their Children, we have unrestricted access to the Throne at any time, to just crawl up onto Their laps, be held by them, and speak to Them about anything. They genuinely do desire to hold us, speak with us, and teach us all things – which is why we were actually created in the first place. I have found that this story helps us to truly understand who we really are, Their relationship to us, and the Authority we have as a Child of the Kingdom. We are a true prince or princess, intentionally made in the Image and Likeness of our Triune LORD GOD; male and female, with a spirit, Soul, and body… three-in-one, just as They are.

This concept is particularly important for us to understand who we are ultimately, and just how precious we are to Them. Remember when Jesus died on the Cross, that the Veil separating us from the Holy of Holies was torn in half, so now we can come boldly to the Throne of Grace at any time. The Death and Blood Sacrifice of Christ Jesus, our Messiah, and our Lord, made that possible.

Always remember this:

You are not alone! You are loved! You have a purpose!

All you have to do is…

# Believe!

---

Now you have a better understanding of who GOD truly is. But, if you have never given your life to GOD and accepted the Free Gift that Jesus, the Son of GOD, made possible by taking on the Death Penalty for us, and giving us a Pardon instead, then I would suggest you repeat this prayer out loud, from your heart…

"Lord Jesus, I know that I am a sinner, and I have broken GOD's Laws. I believe you died for me on the Cross, that I might be saved and set free. I ask for You to Pardon me of all my sins, and that the Holy Spirit would reside within me, to fill the emptiness in my heart, so that I could be in fellowship with You forever. Thank you Jesus, for forgiving all my sins, and giving me Eternal Life. Amen!"

*Romans 10:9-10*
*If you openly declare that "Jesus is Lord" and believe in your heart that GOD raised Him from the dead, you will be saved. For it is by believing in your heart that you are made right with GOD, and it is by openly declaring your Faith that you are saved.*

Printed in Poland
by Amazon Fulfillment
Poland Sp. z o.o., Wrocław
05 July 2023

a0f8f5f7-01f0-4cb7-9eba-7816bc695410R01